OFF COURSE

BY THE SAME AUTHOR

Yemen Rediscovered (*Longman*)
Bahrain: Gulf Heritage in Transition (*Longman*)
Syria in View (*Longman*)
Scotland through the Ages (*Michael Joseph*)
London Heritage (*Michael Joseph*)
A Traveller's Companion to the West Country (*Michael Joseph*)
Journeys into Medieval England (*Michael Joseph*)
Ireland through the Ages (*Michael Joseph*)
The Architectural Heritage of Britain & Ireland (*Michael Joseph*)
Victorian Britain (*Weidenfeld & Nicolson*)
New British Architecture in Germany (*Prestel*)
FlipDesigns (*Prestel*)
FlipSigns (*Prestel*)
Mrs Mulroony's Fly-Away French Bloomers (*Lulu*)
Conundrum's Book (*Lulu*)
Dream of a Summer Night (*Lulu*)
Farthing Abbey (*Lulu*)

OFF COURSE

*Journey of a Wayward Traveller
to the Island of Corsica*

Michael Jenner

ISBN 978-0-9558480-0-1

Copyright © Michael Jenner, 2007

To travel writers past, present and future.

"To travel hopefully is a better thing than to arrive, and the true success is to labour." Robert Louis Stevenson

Poppycock! And balderdash! Sitting here at London Gatwick Airport at 3.47 in the morning I beg to disagree most profoundly with that much loved quote from the godfather of all travel writers Robert Louis Stevenson. Indeed, I would turn the sacred RLS dictum on its head and simply state the opposite. I love being somewhere else even though the act of getting there is generally a pain in the butt.

On the other hand, RLS is much closer to the truth when he talks of the labour involved. For the verb 'travel' has the same root as 'travail' which means to work, as in French *travailler*. The word can also be used to express something unpleasant as in enduring the travails life throws at us. According to the Oxford English Dictionary these can include physical hardship, mental work, various kinds of exertion and suffering or even the pains of childbirth.

So whichever way you look at it, travel is essentially hard graft. And if RLS is right that to arrive is basically a let-down compared to the joys of travel, then that poses an obvious question. What is the point of going there, wherever it is, in the first place?

But all these ruminations still lie a few hours ahead. In terms of strict chronology and narrative sequence I should start this account at the moment I shut the front door behind me and step out into the big wide world. That is the precise point at which the act of travel properly commences. Sedentary man stirs his stumps, waters his geraniums and sets off.

In real life you cannot, at least not yet, be transported in a flash by magic carpet direct to your destination, as seems to happen in most travel books where you find the writer miraculously positioned already on page one in some far-flung country.

Humdrum reality, however, demands that you depart from a place called home. Granted, it may well be possible in the not so distant future to beam yourself to some remote, exotic location, perhaps by attaching yourself to an email and hitting the send button. But with our present technology there are many tiresome hurdles and hoops to jump over and through before there can be any talk of arriving.

So let us wind back the clock from my nocturnal thoughts at Gatwick Airport and begin at the beginning, that is with me poised to leave home.

Wednesday 20 September

Even as I open the front door there's a real buzz in my brain. A sexy tingle runs through my body. Dormant nerves awaken, twitch expectantly. Something is afoot. The familiar routine is about to be broken. Wandering off into the night after dinner instead of winding down for a spot of telly followed by a hot milky drink and a book in bed smacks of illicit pleasure, a tryst with destiny and the big unknown.

So I have to admit there may well be something in the Robert Louis Stevenson 'travel hopefully' dictum after all, though it could be nothing more than just the anticipation of horizons new and the inner release that comes with breaking loose.

At any rate, there is according to the popular cliché a definite spring in my step as I make my fond farewells and leave home, a modest flat in a nicely down-at-heel Edwardian apartment block a stone's throw from Russell Square in central London. It's around 9pm on a mild autumnal Bloomsbury evening as I embark on my several times postponed and much debated journey to Corsica. Why Corsica? Well, I'm not entirely sure actually. Let's come back to that later.

I drag my compact suitcase, a sleek black model no larger than would be required for a long weekend, behind me. Its wheels make clickety-clack sounds in the shallow grooves between the pavement slabs in staccato rhythm rather like a train. It's as if imaginary railway tracks stretch out in front of me.

Meanwhile, to my left I note the gaunt concrete colossus of the Brunswick. This prime 1970s specimen of architectural brutalism is now shedding the scaffolds with which it has been encased for the past year and a half. The developers bill it as the *High Street for Bloomsbury* offering a new urban lifestyle with trendy eateries and designer boutiques. I hope they are right though my recent memories of a London version of a Soviet style *Karl Marx Platz* will not be easily effaced.

I turn the corner into Woburn Place. Not a bus in sight so thankfully there is no unseemly rush to get to the stop. Not that I'm in a particular hurry but there's some stubborn bit of behavioural programming that always has me running to catch a bus or train as if my very life depends on it even when I could equally well wait patiently for the next one.

Tonight, however, I am able to take things calmly for five minutes or so until I see a small convoy of buses heading south in my direction. They are so tightly packed I can't make out the numbers beyond the first. It's a 68, not the one I'm after. I have to make a quick dash to inspect the other two when they all pull in at the stop in tight formation. The second and third are a 168 and a 59, not what I'm after either.

Then a familiar tale unfolds. My bus, a 91, now appears almost out of nowhere. The driver, on seeing the congestion caused by the three stationary buses, decides he really can't be bothered to stop and simply leapfrogs the lot, leaving me fuming. Here I am trying to 'travel hopefully' with all due respect to RLS but I have fallen at the first fence. Instead of enjoying pleasant whimsical thoughts about my journey I'm drafting tetchy emails to the head of Transport for London about bus drivers who hate the travelling public so much they only let them on board as a last resort. I must admit though, if I were driving a double-decker bus, I wouldn't always want to be stopping every few hundred yards just to pick up passengers.

After ten minutes or so the next 91 to Trafalgar Square shows up. This one actually stops and opens its doors just long enough for me to scramble aboard. Then we are off. Unlike its predecessor this one trundles sedately along so I have time to note the Edwardian splendours of Kingsway, Sicilian Avenue and Aldwych. From here we head west along the Strand. I alight at the last stop, Charing Cross.

I've chosen this particular station to add a neat symbolic touch to my departure. This point is as close as it gets to the heart of London. Distances to and from the city centre are measured from a spot just around the corner in Trafalgar Square. There is a great sense of drama here. I really love the way you pass through the portals of a grand old railway hotel and jump on a train that launches itself on a creaky complaining steel bridge across the Thames with great views of St Paul's to the east, Houses of Parliament to the west. There can be no better way to take leave from mother metropolis and strike out for foreign shores.

Please bear with me for wanting to take in and jot down as much as possible just as it occurs to me. Already I realise it will be a daunting task. So I'll have to edit my thoughts even as I think them. There's already far too much to say about everything. The rich historical associations of Charing Cross, for example, could fill a book on their own.

Firstly, there's the cross itself, the present one being a Victorian replica of the original erected by Edward I to mark the last resting place of Queen Eleanor's coffin en route to Westminster Abbey. The king who has the grim epitaph *Hammer of the Scots* engraved on his coffin was in reality also a soft-hearted romantic when it came to his beloved Spanish wife from Castile. So it's good to know that there was more to this man than the one-dimensional basher of Scots.

Next up in my RAM comes Isambard Kingdom Brunel, the greatest of the Victorian engineers, who used the chains from the old Hungerford or Charing Cross Bridge for his masterpiece the Clifton Suspension over the Avon Gorge in Bristol.

Then there's a bit of literary history. Dr Samuel Johnson remarked to Boswell during their discussion with regard to the precise location of London's social epicentre: *"Why, sir, Fleet Street has a very animated appearance: but I think the full tide of human existence is at Charing Cross."* The full tide of human existence is exactly right. For the cast embraces everyone from the rough sleepers under the arches to the lofty personage of General Charles George Gordon.

I invariably think of Gordon when I pass through Charing Cross ever since I learned this was the station from which he set off in January 1884 on his fateful journey to quell the unrest in the Sudan. Gordon was fighting the 19th century equivalent of the War on Terror now being waged in Afghanistan. But things weren't going well for the British forces and Gordon was despatched to rescue the expedition.

It was a hastily concocted mission and Gordon didn't have much by way of administrative or financial resources. So I imagine him on his own kitted out in khaki and pith helmet queuing impatiently for a ticket along with lesser mortals travelling on the semi-fast to Orpington, perhaps even as far as Broadstairs.

When the moustachioed national hero reaches the head of the queue he has to wait a few moments for the cockney ticket clerk Reggie Baldwin to reappear after taking a quick toilet break.

RB: *Now how can I help you, Sir?*

GG: *Khartoum, my good man. And make it snappy. I'm in a bit of a hurry as it happens.*

RB: *Khartoum, Sir?*

GG: *Yes, Khartoum. What do you think I said? You have heard of Khartoum, I trust?*

RB: *Who hasn't heard of Khartoum, Sir? Nasty business. It's in all the papers.*

GG: *Indeed it is.*

RB: *Travelling on our own are we, Sir?*

GG: *Unless you're volunteering to come with me? We need every man we can get. Natives getting restless and all that.*

RB: *Sorry to disappoint, Sir. Used up my annual leave.*

GG: *Forces of extremism have to be confronted, don't you know? No good shirking the responsibility.*

RB: *I'm sure you're right, Sir. So a single to Khartoum it is. Quite sure you don't want a return?*

GG: *No, better make it a single.*

RB: *Are you really sure that's wise, Sir? Sudan not a very good place to settle, in my humble opinion. But there are some nice resorts on the Red Sea …*

GG: *Dammit, man! I'm not going to the Sudan on a bally holiday. Do I look like a tourist? Now just give me a flaming single ticket to Khartoum and get on with it.*

RB: *Tell you what, Sir. For just a bob and three farthings more than the cost of a single you can have a Super Saver Off Peak Return with a free stopover in Cairo, Sir.*

GG: *Hmmm. Under normal circumstances that might be worthy of consideration. But I won't have time for any idle malingering in Egypt. Speed is of the essence, don't you know?*

The softening in Gordon's tone indicates that he like the rest of us is clearly not above being tempted by a cut price special offer. With that, I leave the brave general deliberating over his Sudanese travel options.

As we all know with the benefit of historical hindsight, whichever ticket he actually purchased, his was strictly a one way trip. For Gordon was killed on 26 January 1885, shot by followers of the *Mahdi*, the fundamentalist Islamic leader of the uprising in the Sudan. Gordon's head was paraded on a pike through the streets of Khartoum. Just two days later a British army relief force arrived.

With these images in mind, I picture Gordon's ill-fated train flexing its steel muscles as it shunted remorselessly out of Charing Cross Station blowing steam and wheezing soot-laden coughs like a consumptive with but a few months to live.

In real life I purchase a return ticket to Gatwick Airport and catch a diesel powered *Southern* train, then change at London Bridge for the onward service on *First Capital Connect*. After East Croydon the carriage is almost empty. A solitary man taps away at a laptop with obsessive attention. White neon overhead light bleaches all colour from his face. His suit is an anonymous grey. The garish blue seat upholstery sets my optical nerves on edge. I'm looking at the photographic equivalent of one of Edward Hopper's iconic nocturnal paintings which perfectly encapsulate the isolation, alienation and melancholy of modern life.

Swiftly I draw my digital camera, aim, focus and shoot. Got it! That's Exhibit A as I record the stages of my journey. Man with laptop looks up briefly on account of the shutter noise but doesn't seem bothered. Besides, as in a real Hopper canvas the human being in my picture is only a marginal element, with soul-numbing desolation filling most of the frame. So I don't feel I've invaded his personal privacy.

Even better, the picture is not destined for yet another travel article of the sort that has been my bread and butter for so many years. Having plied my trade as writer and photographer for more than a quarter of a century, I'm ready for a change of routine. Now that

I'm just a couple of stops short of my bus pass it's time to take stock. Every trip I've done for almost as long as I can remember has been for a book, newspaper or magazine. I've forgotten what it's like to be a normal traveller, someone without a commission.

Now the category of normal traveller is not one of those listed by Laurence Sterne in his enigmatic work of 1768 *A Sentimental Journey through France and Italy* though he does offer the following: simple travellers, idle travellers, inquisitive travellers, lying travellers, proud travellers, vain travellers, splenetic travellers and travellers of necessity. He also gives us the delinquent and felonious traveller, the unfortunate and innocent traveller as well as the simple traveller.

At long last Sterne comes to the supreme being of the species, namely the sentimental traveller meaning himself. As for me, I do not think I fit any of the above categories. The closest I can get to a succinct one word description of myself would be wayward. For I'm very much a wayward traveller in the sense of being erratic and following no fixed rule or principle of conduct. In short, my purpose is fluid and ill-defined.

That's the great joy of this particular trip to Corsica. There is no editor expecting me to file a regular and conventional travel story. So for once I can really do my own thing, whatever that is, though that remains to be seen. But why Corsica? I'm afraid I can't answer that yet either. My train is arriving at Gatwick. I must get off or else I'll be travelling south with laptop man to Haywards Heath or Brighton.

Now I've slept over once at Luton and several times at Stansted but Gatwick is an unfamiliar night stop. A quick recce reveals rows of seats at South Terminal and even some without those nasty armrests dividing them. That's great, just what I'm looking for. Means a welcome chance to stretch out and get some serious sleep. Still a few vacant spots available so no great rush. Better have a pee first and buy some mineral water for the night before settling down.

That done, I spot an upper level shopping mall calling itself *Gatwick Village*. Better check that out. You never know. Almost immediately I find exactly what I'm after. I can't believe my luck. A collection of comfy armchairs is scattered about like the contents of a furniture showroom. It's a vaguely undefined area near *Starbucks Coffee*, *Clinton Cards* and several other shops all closed and shuttered for the night.

Only one other person is already installed: a young lad with a Canadian flag on his baseball cap. He is casually spread out between two armchairs forming a very acceptable sofa bed. I devise a similar arrangement and make myself at home. This feels like a class doss. No longer concerned about getting some rest, my main concern now is waking up in time for my flight.

I set the alarm for 4.45am and shut my eyes. But sleep won't come. The BAA (*British Airports Authority*) has conspired to make a night at Gatwick something to be remembered, each single moment of it. Every few minutes one of a random selection of announcements is broadcast at top volume. It's the sort of thing *Amnesty*

International would condemn as noise torture and sleep deprivation.

It begins with: *"Passengers are reminded that in the interests of safety children are not permitted to ride on the baggage trolleys."* OK for adults then? I recall some not so young Italians who whiled away the wee small hours at Stansted Airport staging a modern equivalent of chariot races. Very enjoyable it looked too.

Then there comes the all too familiar: *"For security reasons please do not leave baggage unattended. Baggage left unattended will be removed and may be destroyed."* By far the worst is: *"Passengers, members of the public and staff are advised that the fire alarms ringing in this area are a test procedure. There is no cause for concern."*

There is something vaguely Shakespearian about the way the metallic voice declaims: *"Passengers, members of the public and staff."* Rather like: *"Friends, Romans, countrymen…"* I wonder about the fine and subtle distinction between passengers and members of the public. Are there people now present who are neither working here nor flying somewhere? So who are these members of the public and what's their game?

The fire alarm announcements are doubly annoying because there are in fact no alarm bells ringing and they are delivered like a demented Dalek shouting at Dr Who. What little space there is between these announcements is filled with a medley of mindless jingles as played at Rugby League matches whenever a try is scored. I hear some passengers (or are they members of the public?) make a short-lived fight back singing along karaoke style to the mind-numbing refrain: *"One potato, two potato, three potato, four..."* This mingles with the electronic babble of fruit machines and computer games chatting inanely among themselves: *"... five potato, six potato, seven potato, more."*

This playground mantra has been fiendishly programmed to run on an endless loop. I resolve not to let it get to me. Indeed I must find virtue in living wide awake through what sleep normally protects us from. I try to let my thoughts absorb the prospect of the next few days in Corsica. I shall use the opportunity of this wakeful night in order to morph gradually from whatever I had been before into a proper traveller.

I dismiss the thought that lying slumped in an armchair is hardly the best way to effect the transformation from the sedentary life into that of man on the move. For this I tell myself is no ordinary armchair. It may look like one of those domestic models you find at home but here in the South Terminal of Gatwick Airport it assumes a different personality. Context makes all the difference.

Meanwhile, I observe what cunning ruses my fellow Gatwick night owls are employing to make it through to morning light. Two elderly English ladies sit bolt upright at a table, not one lazy thought of horizontality there. They work their way steadily through a thick book of crossword puzzles. Clearly, they are going to turn night into day by behaving exactly as they would during daylight hours.

Pretending they are at a marathon tea party and denying night its very existence is a bold move, a spirited act of defiance. I salute them. I overhear they are from Eastbourne and have been here since 9pm though their flight is not until 7.20am tomorrow. A middle-aged couple from Manchester likewise look determined to sit it out. But the lady slowly slumps sideways and sheds increasingly intimate articles of clothing as if she were in her own bedroom at home. Meanwhile, her husband stares vacantly into space.

So much for what's going on down our end of the Gatwick dorm.

Thursday 21 September

Around 1am all hope of falling asleep is abandoned when real fire alarms finally start ringing, and ringing and ringing. This creates a group bonding in the face of adversity. Eastbourne speaks unto Manchester and Manchester unto Eastbourne. Bloomsbury lends a sympathetic ear and nods sagely. We are one nation.

I learn that Eastbourne is heading to Faro in the Algarve, preferring Portugal to Spain because it's cleaner and less commercial. Manchester is flying to Swindon. No, that can't be right. It would be quicker to catch a bus. Then I get a clearer signal.

Manchester is going to Lisbon where they have friends. Last year they went to Madeira for their daughter's wedding. The ladies' hat boxes had to be checked in and got all squashed in the hold. But it was alright in the end because the hats survived better than the boxes. Both Eastbourne and Manchester agree it's definitely not worth spending hard-earned cash on an expensive hotel if you're going to have to get up at 3am. I guess Bloomsbury goes along with that too.

The Eastbourne ladies now get back to their crossword puzzles. Inspired by this, I try to devise anagrams of Corsica. Best I come up with is *ARSICOC* which doesn't sound too savoury and *ICCORAS* which is phonetically close to *ICARUS*, mythical symbol of humankind's reckless ambition to go beyond the limits of his earthbound condition.

Mr Manchester is now snoring behind the *Daily Express*. The banner headline reads: *WINTER WILL BE OUR NEW SUMMER*. All about climate change, I guess. Suddenly the *Icarus* legend assumes a new twist. What would the ancient Greeks make of us? Are we getting too big for our boots, flying too close to the sun? Will our wings come unstuck? Is global travel bringing on global disaster?

We certainly live in a global society in that we are all doing our level best to screw the dear old globe for all she's worth. Planet Earth is slowly choking on toxic gases from thousands and thousands of aeroplanes girdling the earth for the sole purpose of transporting humans on journeys of little or no consequence. So am I another nasty little eco-vandal by doing this two hour flight to Corsica? I am reminded of the title of a Paul Gauguin Tahitian painting that translates as *"Where do we come from? What are we? Where are we going?"* To which I might add: *"What on earth are we doing?"*

But the big thought occupying me is about time, or rather *the* time. I watch it tick away with agonising slowness. TUE20 takes ages to become WED21 on the date panel of my watch. It's not yet 2am and I'm sure there isn't one of us dossing down in *Gatwick Village* who wouldn't happily fast forward to 6am and toss four hours of human life in the trash can just to get out of this zombie-like state of suspended animation. I know it's a crime to wish time to shrink and I also realise that's a wise old granny of a reflection. But these are mental reflexes I can't stop in the wee small hours.

Gatwick Village, now that's a thought. There was once upon a time a tiny Sussex hamlet of that name probably known to not very many people outside the immediate locality. The same applies to the formerly rustic villages of Heathrow and Stansted. Through some act of magic engineered by the vagaries of airport planning these obscure, utterly forgettable places have become names of global renown.

Just when I think sleep will never come again, finally it does. For suddenly I awake to discover the clock has moved on to 03.47. That makes it definitely tomorrow. Neck may be stiff, mouth dry and head fuzzy but there's a huge sense of triumph, almost over time itself. Eastbourne and Manchester look pretty pleased with themselves too. We've come through the worst, broken the back of the beast. BAA has done its worst to keep us from sleeping, but we've beaten the BAAstards! Sorry about that, chaps. Only joking.

Check-in for my 07.15 flight to Bastia should open at 04.45, now less than an hour away. Might as well get myself together and saunter over to North Terminal. I take a nostalgic farewell picture of the faithful armchair that has carried me safely through the night. Exhibit B, as I continue to record my progress.

Now the rest is a doddle. Even the coiling queue to check-in moving at a snail's pace and as densely packed as the Chicago stockyards can be endured. The departure lounge is yet another bland shopping mall.

Impossible to imagine Gatwick is really an airport with actual planes waiting somewhere behind the scenes to carry us up and away. I am mesmerised by the tackiness of a mind-boggling shop called *GLORIOUS BRITAIN*. Just to confirm it's not a hallucination I take a snap of a life-size plastic beefeater yeoman warden. This is 21st century Britain: phoney heritage in a mock medieval uniform. Exhibit C.

"Passengers on BA6772 to Bastia can now proceed to gate 52." I make haste in that direction. One last picture opportunity before boarding the plane is of the horrendous carpet pattern. So awful it's actually a work of art. That's Exhibit D and from now on I won't be making a note of every single picture I take.

Once inside the aircraft my professional past catches up with a vengeance and for the next couple of hours there'll be no escape. I haven't been on a BA plane since I was a regular contributor to a British Airways in-flight magazine called *Business Life*. Over a heady five years I flew at least fifty assignments all over the European network: from Madeira to Moscow, Manchester to Marrakech. Sorry about the excessive alliteration: an old travel writer's habit, I'm afraid.

These trips were essentially lightning raids. Jet in, get the material and fly home even before I realised I was somewhere else. It was the journalistic equivalent of smash-and-grab. But not like a common thief more a superior purloiner of jewellery always staying in the best hotels and dining at the most expensive restaurants, invariably on the house. I soon forgot what it was like to have to ask for a bill, let along pay one. It was loads of fun and I had the time of my life. So when the circus finally ran its course I had this feeling of being left high and dry. Then after a while I realised I wasn't altogether unpleased to be off the treadmill.

Still I can't resist a nostalgic peek at the in-flight reading. There's *High Life*, rather thinner than I remember it, as if starved of advertising. Perhaps it's on a trendy diet? There's no sign of *Business Life*. In its place, I discover a fat glossy magazine calling itself *Med Life* which seems to be flourishing. As the title conveys, *Med Life* covers the Mediterranean network operated by GB Airways on behalf of BA.

I scan a feature about Michael Palin with the heading: *TEA AND EMPATHY*. Nice title for a nice story on a nice man. MP explains over a friendly cuppa that he prefers rubbing shoulders with the locals to visiting museums and monuments, and rates street food and simple eateries over posh places with Michelin stars. In fact, the very opposite to the 5 star treatment that became my lot. So hats off to you, Michael. You certainly brought travelogues down to earth.

But there's something that niggles about the phenomenon of Palin's travels, I mean as seen on TV. The programmes present us with images of a friendly Englishman abroad on a solo mission greeting all and sundry with spontaneous natural ease. We are beguiled into overlooking the fact that the whole thing is a sophisticated BBC TV production. Getting sufficient footage of MP doing his natural and spontaneous thing must mean that the cameraman is constantly on the look-out for likely situations if not actually setting them up. What if the first take isn't quite right? Do they re-shoot until they get it spontaneous enough?

Of the top flight travel writers, Colin Thubron springs to mind as a genuine one man show. Whether scampering around in the hills of Lebanon, going upcountry in China or tramping along the Silk Road, CT delivers the goods in an honest and dare I say old fashioned manner. He really does fly solo, gets his boots dirty, takes you to the coalface of the journey and tells of real human encounters, while whisking you off periodically into erudite areas of philosophy, history and mythology. His keen descriptive eye takes the place of photography. Like a fastidious Victorian watercolorist he will faithfully and painstakingly give you in precise brushstrokes as much as his verbal palette can supply. In short, *Château Thubron* is regarded by many as the *Grand Cru Classé* of the genre.

There was a time I would have liked to make long, lonely journeys describing everything in painterly prose. I once found myself in an ideal position to flex my travel writer's muscles when I journeyed for ten days through northern Thailand with a Buddhist monk, sleeping rough on the teak planks of temple floors, eating food offered by the local people.

That particular jaunt occurred as an unscripted side trip during a round-the-world-in-thirty-days air trip. Only afterwards did I think to write it up. During my stopover in Singapore I bought a *Hermes Baby* portable typewriter, the 1981 equivalent of the *Mac Powerbook*, to record my experiences. I pounded the keys for a couple of days while the monsoon did its worst.

The resulting pages were never submitted to any publisher. To be frank, they didn't cut the mustard. Apart from the fact that the trip was too short for a big book, I discovered that my mind was too superficial for the task of the serious travelogue. I am indeed too wayward, too much of a gadfly. I'd find it impossible to last even half a day on the *Silk Road* without some irreverent observation creeping in to undermine the whole enterprise. Not to mention my lack of real traveller guts to tough it out it in difficult places.

So much for past aspirations, Corsica now comes into view on starboard and I'm extremely well placed to take it all in. But excitement is followed by big panic. How can I describe it? Well, the island looks rocky, mountainous even. There's a great tangle of blue remembered hills set in a wine dark sea under a haze of cloud, with a backdrop of jagged peaks offering a hint of Mordor. Well, there are a few descriptive touches plundered from Dennis Potter, Homer and J.R.R. Tolkein respectively just to get things started.

There's a decidedly crablike shape to the bay down there. I mean a crab's claw rather than a whole crab of course. Or maybe a lobster's claw would be more accurate? I'll have to check. The sea displays a miraculously radiant turquoise at the white sandy edges merging tastefully into a deeper, darker aquamarine further out. Bit like a travel poster. No that doesn't do the trick. Oh, what is the secret of using words to evoke visual matters? Better take a photo for now and hope to get some verbal inspiration later.

Describing colour is a tricky business. No-one has given it a better shot than A.S. Byatt in *The Matisse Stories*. Absolutely brilliant, real *tour de force*, though in less expert hands such as my own things might end up reading like a *Dulux* paint chart without the colour samples. How many words, for example, are there for shades of brown? Mud, tobacco, chocolate, coffee (all shades from *espresso* to *café au lait*), amber, hemp, tan, leather, acorn, beechnut, wood, dung, manure etc. Sprinkle a few over your landscape, *et voilà!*

Now it's final approach. At this point I have to admit to having mixed feelings about islands. The powerful attraction to them is rapidly followed by an equally powerful urge to get off them and a morbid fear of entrapment. I must have some deep-seated dread of being stranded. For the relief I experience on leaving an island usually surpasses the elation I felt on arrival. Now automatically, I consult my travel notes to make sure my exit routes are in place. Yes, there are sufficient flights and ferries from all three places I'll be visiting over the next five days: Bastia, Ajaccio and Calvi.

Something about these names catches my eye. It takes me a moment to rearrange the initials into ABC, the first three letters of the alphabet. Bingo! That's it, the title for my story: *Corsican ABC*. Just the sort of silly nonsense so beloved of travel editors, at least in the English-speaking world. Only in this case it might actually have a real meaning in that Ajaccio, Bastia and Calvi, just like the abbreviation ABC, will stand in for the full alphabet of the Corsican experience.

However, I won't be ticking them off in strict alphabetical order. I'm starting in Bastia, going on to Ajaccio and Calvi, then back to Bastia. So it'll be more a case of B, A, C, B. That could be the opening notes of a tune. It also occurs that Corsica may have entered the English language through the word 'corsair', which I see as a better class of pirate or pirate ship from the Barbary Coast, a cut above the average buccaneer.

Only a few seconds to touchdown, so let me quickly say that I can't go with the *Corsican ABC* title since this account of my journey to Corsica is not really about Corsica in any meaningful sense. I'll stick with an earlier idea: *Off Course*. This was originally *Off Corse* but then I wondered if some people would see the French word for Corsica as a typo. So *Off Course* it is, and a clear winner over *Corsican ABC* since it also speaks for my own waywardness, general lack of direction and the dire state of the world today.

So this account comes with a health warning. If you want something useful and actually on the subject of Corsica then I can thoroughly recommend the *Insight Guide* for an overall impression in words and pictures to prepare for the trip. But as a travel companion I'm taking the invaluable *Rough Guide* with me. Many snippets of information I quote in these pages have been garnered from this source. In fact, RG is a perfect companion in many ways with a journalist's eye for what's relevant and newsworthy, plus handy hints for where to eat and drink. In fact, I've come to regard RG as a real person and at times I find myself sharing thoughts with him rather than writing them down.

I'm scribbling this in my reporter's notebook as the plane hits the tarmac, bringing me up with a sharp jolt. I now remind myself that since I have no writing commission there's no need for me to agonise over titles and suchlike. So I really don't have to bother with any of that. I can just do my own thing for my own private reasons. Art for art's sake. Wasn't that what I wanted a very long time ago?

Suddenly, I feel quite naked, devoid of purpose. The folly of what I am doing hits hard. I am reminded of Dr Johnson's cruel dictum: *"No man but a blockhead wrote for any reason except money."* Well, sir, I am that blockhead. What's more, I am paying my own way as well. How about that for the height of folly?

On the other hand that leaves me free to follow my fancy, do whatever comes into my head. I don't have to write another word. Or I can write as many as I wish. In fact, I can write myself out thoroughly, empty the tanks, flush the tubes, purge the system, perform a mega dump, if you'll pardon the expression. And what I write is under no obligation to be a literal description of the physical place Corsica. In short, I have come here not to extract material out of Corsica but to allow Corsica to extract material out of me. *Voilà la différence!*

I'm glad I have that sorted in my head just as the plane comes to a halt a short distance from the terminal. I would prefer to walk but we must take a big bendy bus to get there. Hooded crows patrol the concrete apron, dark-suited *mafiosi* in black jackets with grey waistcoats keeping a watchful eye on us to make sure we don't stray. I wait impatiently for the 20 second ride across 100 meters of tarmac to the baggage hall.

My small suitcase finally turns up. It looks rather inconsequential alongside many more serious items of luggage. I could have taken it on board but for the new security regulations. Apart from that I have a compact camera bag with a side pocket for travel docs. I want to travel light, move fast as and when needed, not draw attention to myself, blend in with surroundings, a bit like a spy. Keep calm. Be cool.

I make what might easily have been a fatal error right after Customs by stopping for a pre-emptive pee. A formidable *Madame* guards the downstairs loo and I have no small change for her china saucer. What's more she wants to look after my suitcase too as part of the service. While figuring out how I'm going to make a dignified exit it occurs to me I might easily miss the bus into town during the time spent splashing my boots. Now I'm suddenly man in a hurry, no longer calm and cool as I make haste to leave the urinal.

The bus approaches just as I emerge from the terminal. I catch it by the skin of my teeth. The driver informs me that if I had missed this one, I'd have to wait 2 hours and 40 minutes for the next.

"*Oui, monsieur. Deux heures et quarante minutes.*"

He's remarkably proud of this gaping black hole in the timetable and points emphatically to a printed notice to confirm matters. It's true. There's nothing at all between the 11.05 and the 13.45. But surely this is meant to be a shuttle? The driver then explains in melodic French laced with a dash of Italian that since the airport bus is subsidised by individual airlines it only connects with their flights. As it happens, BA alias GB Airways hasn't paid its dues so passengers arriving from London must take pot luck. It seems I have been very lucky indeed that our flight coincided with one from Paris or Marseille. I make a mental note to double-check vital travel facts, and take nothing for granted.

I enjoy the bus ride into town. The approaches to Bastia are not half as bad as RG would have me believe. With no spinning taxi meter to take the shine off proceedings, I sit back and happily watch the world go by. I'm so relaxed I nod off. Suddenly, here we are pulling up in front of *La Préfecture*. End of the line. We're here. Downtown Bastia. Let Corsica begin.

Before disembarking I ask the driver about the bus connecting with my return flight at 09.50 on Tuesday morning. A triumphant smile cracks his face as he stabs once more at the timetable.

"Vous voyez ça? Rien du tout entre le 6.10 et le 9.15."

It doesn't take me long to work out that the first means getting up at the crack of dawn and getting there three hours too early; and the second arriving at the airport just in time to watch my plane take off.

But surely I'm meant to be exploring Corsica not already planning my exit. Right now, there's a railway journey to be sorted. I make a hash of buying my train ticket to Ajaccio where I'll be spending the first two nights. Rather like General Gordon I ask for just a single, only to remember a minute later there might also be the option of a cheap railway pass valid for all journeys during my stay.

So I return to the counter to enquire if I can start all over again. The ticket clerk kindly does the sums for me and confirms yes I would be better off with a *Carte Zoom* even for the three trips I have planned. He then takes back my ticket, hands me a *Carte Zoom* and I pay the difference. Simple as that. So far two very pleasant Corsicans. I take this as a good omen.

Bastia gets its name from Italian *bastilgia* as in French *bastille* and the city knows a thing or two about invaders and occupiers. The crumbling skyscraper tenements of the old town were built during the long period of Genoese occupation. For many centuries until 1796 Bastia was an Italian fiefdom. Since then, along with the rest of Corsica, it has been officially a part of metropolitan France. So Corsica is not a French colony, I hasten to add, though it may sometimes feel that way with the violent antipathy of certain citizens to many things Gallic. As for language, Corsican dialect is an earthy unique mix of Italian and French. So much for history and linguistics. I'm hungry.

First I must get rid of this suitcase. But there is no *consigne* at the station. So I drag it down to the *Office de Tourisme* on the main square where I am told there may be some private enterprise a few blocks away that will take care of my luggage. Trouble is it's in the wrong direction for what I want to do in the two and a half hours before my train. Somehow I don't feel like a leisurely lunch with my suitcase for company, so eating goes on hold while I get the measure of Bastia.

Place St Nicolas is an amazingly big public arena for a small town of 40,000 people. Its broad acres are big enough to drill an army. Right now with not many people about it feels like an empty parade ground. The hard asphalt surface makes few concessions. If it had one of those nice hard packed sandy surfaces which the French often use in their public gardens then at least the *boules* players could have some fun here and give the square a human dimension. But I am impressed by the huge ocean going vessels moored along the east side of the square that gives directly onto the sea.

As it is, the only person hanging about today is Napoleon Bonaparte skimpily dressed up like a Roman emperor in a rather fetching off-the-shoulder toga. The sculptor has gone to a lot of trouble with the torso, endowing *Boney* with nicely tuned stomach muscles. He may not have the full six pack by today's standards, though it looks like he has been working out.

RG considers the statue to be tad camp and I am not going to argue with that. I can indeed see a distinct leaning towards Michelangelo's *David*. It conveys the same blend of youthful arrogance with just a flicker of self-doubt behind the eyes. But even the great man doing his star turn and flexing his pecs in dazzling white marble on a lofty plinth rattles around a bit in the wide open expanse of *Place St Nicolas*.

    I hadn't bargained for such an early encounter with the most famous Corsican of all time. I wonder if the statue is a backhanded tribute to Napoleon. After all he was born in the rival town of Ajaccio which he elevated to capital of Corsica at Bastia's expense. So I had Napoleon filed under A for Ajaccio which is where I'll be spending the next couple of days, that is if I don't miss my train now just a couple of hours away.

    Glancing at my watch, I reflect on the flexible quality of time. It is not a constant. Two hours spent in the middle of the night at Gatwick Airport feels like a life sentence. But the same amount of time for checking out the major sights of an unknown city runs through my fingers like sand.

    I press on to *Place du Marché*. Thank heavens there is no market. I hate having to snap them for magazines. Getting in the faces of working people trying to go about their business is not the best way to endear oneself to the locals. In the past you could risk a few gruff remarks and some appropriate body language. Now it's swung too far the other way with market holders posing cheesily to camera and holding up their produce as if they expect to be on the front cover of a glossy magazine. Or perhaps they think I might know someone who knows Michael Palin and they'll be on prime time TV. As I said, thank heavens the market is closed. I can imagine it all.

Next stop, the *Vieux Port*. There is real drama as I duck and weave through narrow twisting alleys and vaulted passageways where those towering medieval tenements built by the Genoese block out the sun. The area has a bit of a reputation. You might well fear for your person in this stewing hugger-mugger of an urban labyrinth where all manner of villains could operate with impunity.

I recall too late the stark warnings in the *Insight Guide* about Corsican cities: *"pickpockets and car thieves are rampant; many use motorbikes for a speedy snatch and getaway …. increase in juvenile crime over the past few years is noticeable … not merely a matter of petty offences … increasingly by organised gangs of thieves."*

Sounds lively to say the least. But in the event the reality as I experience it is that you can no longer rely on getting even a half decent mugging in downtown Bastia. You would think a hapless foreigner such as myself, touting a reasonably expensive digital camera and with a tidy wad of euros in his money belt, would be a sitting duck at the mercy of any idle felon or miscreant. Yet I emerge untroubled and unscathed.

At first sight the *Vieux Port* glimpsed like the light at the end of a tunnel gets my pulse racing. I imagine it smaller but with more ambiance than Marseille and probably not yet gentrified. Moments later, as I blink expectantly in the bright sunshine I immediately realise I'm at least ten years too late. No colourful fishing boats just the white fibre glass of yachts and motor cruisers occupying every inch of water while parked cars have taken over the quays.

Am I alone in finding marinas death to the soul? The new purpose built ones at least have modernity writ large all over them but when an ancient harbour gets made over into a *port de plaisance* it's as shocking as caravans blighting a medieval town square. Can you imagine artists and painters getting inspiration from all that plastic, chrome and stainless steel?

But the setting is pretty good and the sun is shining from just the right angle. So the dutiful travel photographer, albeit uncommissioned, draws camera from bag and sets about coaxing the most flattering portrait out of this motley scene. I even locate one or two older craft that have some appeal and frame a shot around them. I'm quite pleased with my efforts though I feel uneasy about doing my dishonest bit to make the *Vieux Port* look far more atmospheric than she is.

Meanwhile, any thoughts of lunch at some salty waterfront dive are long gone. It's all spruced up with *restaurants touristiques* announcing *formule* this or *formule* the other. I decide I will give the *Vieux Port* a second try on my last day when I'll be spending a night in town.

Another glance at my watch. Only an hour and a half before I have to be back at the station. My progress is now blocked by the vertical mass of the Citadel. Under the hot sun, on an empty stomach and with a suitcase in tow I'm no match for the great staircase leading up through the *Jardin Romieu*. So I retrace my steps to *Place St Nicolas* thinking now of a quick snack and a drink in one of the *grands cafés*.

Then I am distracted by something that appears to be trapped in a complete time warp: a wonderful Art Deco commercial premises complete with faded hand-painted advertisements and crumbling relief. This is the drinks emporium of Louis Napoleon Mattei maker of the famous *Cap Corse* aperitif, a concoction of quinine, Muscat and orange peel created in 1872 and still going strong. Well, strongish.

For *Cap Corse*, once a national brand, languished and all but disappeared in the post-war period. Since 1981, however, a group of young Corsicans have been busy relaunching the business. They opened up a new factory but so far are resisting any temptation to renovate their original downtown premises which still feature ceiling-high glass cabinets containing ancient distillations in old bottles like apothecary's jars.

I ask permission to photograph, which is politely given, and so I have a happy time extracting nostalgic images. Countless faces of Napoleon Bonaparte stare impassively forth from rows of bottles. I make a mental note to sample this most Corsican of drinks.

Mon Dieu! It's 3pm. Can it be that late already? Barely half an hour left in Bastia so only the quickest of bites for lunch will have to do. En route to the station I resort to a self-service cafeteria where I devour a Corsican lasagne and local beer. From a small shop I grab a bottle of mineral water and today's paper for the journey. I get back to the station with just enough time to examine the exhibition panels on display.

It's all to do with the extensive engineering works and major renovations currently in progress on the *Chemins de Fers Corses* network. New rolling stock is on order and doubtless it will be a traveller's dream in approximately three years time. The bad news is that this refurbishment will necessitate periodic closures. So passengers are kindly asked to note that a replacement rail bus service will be operating between Ponte Leccia and Ajaccio.

I groan from the depths of my being. The sinuous mountain line over to the west coast is rated by the *cognoscenti* to be the most spectacular stretch of rail in Corsica. There are train spotters who would think it worth coming all the way here just for that. Still at least I will get to leave Bastia pulled by a smelly old diesel and chug along for about an hour to the junction at Ponte Leccia where we must de-train and en-bus.

I spend the few minutes prior to departure making notes of the various *graffiti* I've spotted so far: *LINGUA CORSA LINGUA VIVA. LIBERTA. PARIS GANG. CORSA SEMPRE IN LOTTA.*

Evidently, there is still a fair amount of unappeased Corsican nationalist sentiment. To confirm matters, today's edition of *Corse-Matin* in its regular *VIOLENCE* column reports a couple of bomb scares at a disused holiday camp. Fortunately, these turned out to be a hoax. More sinister was a very real drive-past shoot-up of a café right here in Bastia. This is presumed a racist attack since it injured several Moroccan regulars. The weapons used were paintball guns where the capsules had been replaced by something more solid.

That happened a whole week ago and it's only been reported today. Scene of the crime was near *Place du Marché* where I was strolling just now thinking how safe and peaceful. I can't put this down exactly as a near miss, but it's certainly registered on my radar. So I'm quite happy not to be spending my first night in Bastia. Instead I'm taking it in two bites: today being a kind of appetiser with the main course to follow on Monday.

Another news item to catch my eye concerns the US Navy base at La Maddalena on neighbouring Sardinia. According to an Italian naval officer American submarines have for years been dumping radioactive waste water from their nuclear reactors into the sea between Corsica and Sardinia. Accordingly, there is a fear that some Corsican waters have been dangerously polluted including the *International Marine Park of Bonifacio* at the far south of the island. I do hope it's not true but I have a dark feeling it may be.

Not for the first time Corsica finds herself at the business end of the American military. There was a ghastly friendly fire incident in Bastia during the Second World War. RG tells the story most succinctly.

"On the day after the island's liberation in 1943, a squadron of B52s belatedly launched an aerial attack against the nonexistent Germans, von Senger and Etterlin's Ninth Panzer Division having already completed its withdrawal across the Ligurian Sea. With many people in the streets celebrating the

retreat, civilian casualties exceeded the total sustained throughout the occupation and many old buildings were destroyed, including much of the old governor's palace; the consequences of the bombing can still be seen in Terra Vecchia (the Old Town)."

I am tempted to write *plus ça change* by way of a mischievous footnote, and indeed I have.

Right on time the train pulls out of Bastia and immediately we plunge into a long tunnel. As we rattle along in the dark I am reminded powerfully of the London Underground. I wouldn't be surprised if, when we pop out into daylight, our little train of two carriages pulls in at the Piccadilly Line platform at Barons Court. Furiani is our next stop. This name has me reaching once more for RG who resumes his commentary.

"However, the worst tragedy since the war occurred on May 5, 1992 when a stand in the Furiani Stadium, home of Corsica's top football team Sporting Club de Bastia, collapsed during a European Cup tie with arch rivals Olympic de Marseille. Seventeen supporters died in the disaster and more than 1300 were injured. Those responsible have yet to be brought to justice, while the issue of compensation for the victims has become embroiled in scandal and protracted legal cases."

At this point you might well be wondering if I intend unashamedly to pad out my own account with great chunks of the *Rough Guide* by David Abram. The answer is a firm no. I quote those two passages in their entirety rather than paraphrase and seek to pass them off as my own in order to convey the nice journalistic flavour that puts RG in a class of its own.

I glance back to Furiani now disappearing behind us down the tracks. Although there is a spanking new stadium ghosts yet to be laid to rest hover still.

We stop briefly at Casamozza. The very name is so redolent of Mediterranean warmth and the Italian Deep South. It's also a graveyard for ancient Corsican Railways rolling stock that has rolled its last into these rusty, overgrown sidings. If only I had even five minutes, I could do some great pictures of this poetic scene of industrial dereliction smouldering in the sunshine. Alas, we are only here for a moment and so there's no chance to alight. I must content myself with a quick gaze through the smeary windows.

The vintage carriages sport a lovely faded red and gold two tone livery like that of the old *S-Bahn* in Berlin. This once classy metropolitan railway remained the property and responsibility of the East German socialist regime long after the city was divided. Hardly a Pfennig was spent on it for forty years or so until the Wall came down. The train I am now riding in is painted white with some wishy-washy blue stripes making it look more like a caravan or mobile home.

After Casamozza the scenery gets markedly more dramatic. The rugged mountainous spine of Corsica rears up all covered in dense shrub known as the *maquis*. This landscape provided a superb natural cover into which during the last war members of the Corsican resistance melted away making it impossible for the Germans to pursue them. The Corsican *maquis* became a legend for the impregnability of its refuges so that the word came to stand for the very spirit and emblem of the French Resistance. *Le maquis* was adopted as the name of the movement even in mainland France, a place to which Corsicans refer not without irony as if to a remote foreign country as *le continent*.

The other special property of the *maquis* is its heady perfume of aromatic herbs which deliver a truly powerful hit causing noses to crinkle in anticipation of dishes like *entrecôte grillée aux herbes du maquis*. Napoleon, not generally know for any nostalgic fondness for Corsica, could still be guided back to his roots it was said by the enchanting whiff of the *maquis*. It only took his nose to tell him he was home. All I can smell right now is the good old railway pong of oil and diesel.

I make a right mess of things at Ponte Leccia, the junction where we have to change from train to bus for the onward journey to Ajaccio. The afternoon sun caresses a wonderful old station building, its many times plastered façade flaking off in gorgeous multi-layered shades of pink, yellow and orange. Ghostly grey letters spelling out BUFFET are barely visible as if they might fade away before the day is out.

Before I know it I am out of the train and about to cross the tracks. Then I spot a fellow passenger, a young lady with a small infant son and an enormous rucksack who looks like she needs a hand. So back I go to the train. But she's doing fine. Then I think I'll dump my case in the waiting bus so I'll have a free hand for the snaps. I ask the driver if we have a few minutes to spare. "*Oui. Oui. Allez-y.*" But then *le contrôleur* turns up and suddenly it's cries of all aboard; and off we go.

All I can do is look back wistfully over my shoulder at the receding prospect of those lovely images dissolving like a dream before my eyes. I know I'll be passing through Ponte Leccia twice more before this trip is over. Though the light is bound to be different and with it the entire mood.

To cap it all I didn't even render assistance to the lady. So from being a contented train traveller suddenly I am a disgruntled bus passenger. I now think long and hard about the rail journey I'm missing. So what exactly is it about trains? I mean trains as opposed to buses, rail rather than road. Wherein lies the magic of the one and the banality of the other? A train rattling along on rails and whistling around bends is the stuff of poetry. To wax lyrical about a bus ride simply doesn't work. It's not remotely in the same league.

Somehow, trains leave behind the familiar scene of streets and junctions, service stations and suchlike. We get to see back gardens rather than front doors. In a train we enter a virgin landscape, vanish up a valley with no company but ourselves, the outside world glimpsed through a window framing the view like a cinema screen. Yes, it's like watching a movie, at one remove from mundane reality. In short, everything looks subtly but essentially different when seen from a train.

Throughout the two hour ride from Ponte Leccia to Ajaccio road and rail follow the same convoluted route through the mountains. I keep a watchful eye on the iron tracks and viaducts to imagine what I might be seeing. At times we run parallel, but occasionally, while the road takes a few hairpin bends to gain altitude the railway takes a short cut through a tunnel only to re-appear smugly way ahead of us.

These trivial observations lift my spirits. The fact that I'm in a bus no longer bothers me. I'm having more than an *ersatz* train experience. Any lingering disgruntlement vanishes, leaving me in a state for which I struggle to find a word. How about gruntlement? Yes, the word hits the spot as I get the hang of gruntling or being in this rare and delightful mood of feeling good for no apparent reason.

Meanwhile, my mind continues to occupy itself figuring out what views I would be having from the train. Generally speaking, decidedly better I reckon, but at several places surprisingly it's the bus that enjoys the grandstand seat. So time passes pleasurably enough with road and rail performing a long-distance tango in which the road is definitely the female being obliged to make many more turns and swirls around the steadier course of the railway. Finally both come together and swoop down in tandem towards the finishing line.

Then finally the dance is done and the music stops. The bus comes to a shuddering halt on a parking lot right by the train platforms. We get to disembark through the station building. So I reckon I've had two journeys for the price of one. You could call my mood one of supreme gruntlement, as at around a quarter to seven on a balmy September evening I enter Ajaccio.

I trundle my suitcase a few hundred yards up the main drag of *Cours Napoléon* bustling with people and traffic to *Hôtel Kallisté* where I have booked a room via an internet reservation system. It's only a 2 star but this is how I used to travel many years ago before the seductive luxuries that come with professional travel writing were strewn across my path.

I step into the tight confines of room 307 like a monk entering his spartan cell. There is nothing surplus to requirements, with everything pared down to the absolute minimum, but clean and acceptable for all that. For the next two nights this tiny walled box will be my home, my private space and personal universe too.

They've even economised on the view for when I push open the shutters there's nothing to see but a blank wall of other shutters staring back at me with blinkered eyes. I think of Jean-Paul Sartre's play *Huis Clos* which translates literally as closed shutters, though *No Exit* is the title of the English version. The point I'm trying to make is that no one does closed shutters better than the French. They really do shut you out while shutting in all manner of private and possibly dark material. For conformity's sake I opt to keep my shutters shut. I may only be a two night stand in a two star hotel but there are standards to maintain.

First I need a shower. I kick off my clothes. My stale T-shirt and crumpled boxer shorts lie on the tiled floor like the discarded skin of a snake. What a nuisance having to cart dirty underwear about and take it home. How nice it would be to have disposable items to be dropped and discarded along the way. I've been wearing this set for 24 hours since stepping out in Bloomsbury yesterday evening although it feels like a lot longer. I get instant refreshment under a long, warm shower and judicious application of a thin translucent bar of *savon végétal* courtesy of *Hôtel Kallisté*.

I am pleased to discover that the name *Kallisté* is from Greek, as the omniscient RG informs in the opening lines of his guidebook, and it means 'most beautiful', a reference to the fulsome description accorded to Corsica by an anonymous ancient Greek travel writer. Wonder if he was on a press trip?

'Most beautiful' is precisely how I feel, if not how I look, as I dry off. My skin tingles like that of a new borne babe. The sensation is not just physical. I've washed off something else as well. My travel fatigue has vanished. I'm fresh and raring to go, really quite excited to be here and interested in absolutely everything as if I've arrived from a different planet.

Even without leaving my hotel room there's plenty to keep me busy, like the colour scheme of the bathroom for example. The oxblood red ceramic tiles and matching porcelain crapper crowned with a pink plastic lid are just screaming for Matisse to do a portrait of an *odalisque à sa toilette*. For want of an artist's model I shoot the scene as an abstract, still life composition, but it still packs quite a punch.

I'm now ready to venture forth. A glance at the Ajaccio city map reveals that half of the streets have some sort of Napoleonic reference. But I'll take the full

Bonaparte hit tomorrow. I chose a restaurant with a name as far removed from the experience as you could wish. *Don Quichotte* in the heart of the old town also comes well recommended by RG as a place where the locals love to tuck in to their steaks although the fish is 'invariably delicious' too. My problem is that much as I like fish there is something about a rare steak dripping blood that really gets the juices flowing.

Modern humanity in the form of *homo sapiens* took a defining evolutionary step when meat was added to the vegetarian menu of grass, herbs, fruit etc that had nourished us along with the rest of the primates. So I'm always tugged in the direction of *viande*, which in French originally meant food in general, the word being derived ultimately from Latin *vivere* 'to live'. So meat has a lot going for it and this, added to my preference for red wine over white, naturally gives me plenty to think about while studying the menu.

The waiter has circled a couple of times. I sense this is his final approach as he bears down on me, pad in hand. Stalling for time I ask the first question that pops into my head. What is the *plat du jour*? He patiently repeats what is chalked on the board in front of me: *lieu à l'ajacienne* which is pollack cooked in the local style with red peppers and served on a bed of rice. I hear myself ordering the *lieu* and a half bottle of house red. I am still dreaming of that steak perhaps.

What tipped things in favour of the fish is its local preparation. I'm always a sucker for that. Plus the fact that we are by the sea. By the sea? Suddenly I remember the story in *Corse-Matin* about the US Navy pumping radioactive waste into the Med. But it's too late to change my order and I'm reassured by the chap at the next table also ordering the *lieu* though a different version with a creamy basil sauce.

Thoughts start to flow as I take in my surroundings. Over the bar there's a youthful picture of Che Guevara, not the usual shot as on a million T-shirts but a less familiar pose that has me looking twice just to make sure I've identified him correctly. Beneath Che, and yes it is him, a lithe Corsican lady pours the wine and shakes the cocktails. She wears tight-fitting faded blue jeans and a skimpy top revealing an olive skinned midriff. Occasionally she sallies forth on some errand or other, skipping nimbly between the tables, light-footed as a schoolgirl playing hopscotch.

I'm just polishing off the *salade romaine* starter when my wayward eye registers a brilliant flash of red. What was that? It's gone before I know it. Two minutes later there it is again. This time I recognise it as a minuscule scarlet thong just peeping up intermittently above the lady's denim waistband like a tiny exotic bird peering out between the leaves of a rainforest. Now you see it, now you don't. The *lieu à l'ajacienne* is appetising enough but my mind is no longer on my plate. Dinner at *Don Quichotte* has been upstaged by an unscripted floorshow as erotic as *Le Moulin Rouge*.

I cool off afterwards with a walk towards the port. Not many people about though it's not too late, only 10pm or so. As a photographer, one of the things I used to like about night was I could stop taking pictures: absolutely no point without a tripod and awful with flash so I hardly bothered. Digital cameras have changed all that. Just boost the film speed and you get nocturnal shots of very decent quality. So now I cart my camera bag around at all times. You never know.

I'm looking at a brightly lit café-bar, not a great shot in itself but the name of the establishment has caught my eye: *L'IDÉAL*. Can you imagine an English pub or tea room calling itself *THE IDEAL*? Clearly the French are on a completely different wavelength in matters of the mind to come up with something abstract like that. Yet also how unlike them at the same time, since bars in France generally have harmless, simple names like *Rendez-vous des Amis* and *Café du Marché* or *Bar des Sports*. But there it is picked out against a backdrop of bright white neon: *L'IDÉAL*.

I take the shot, not a great one, framing the whole building from the pavement tables right up to the night sky. In the process I've attracted what looks like unwelcome attention. A lady on the café terrace tosses a comment in my direction that I can't quite make out. It has to be something to with the picture I've just taken. I explain the broad lines of my composition concluding with the remark in French along the lines of: *"Don't worry. I wasn't snapping you."*

Fortunately she's nicely oiled with drink and not meaning anything much as she tells me she would have been far happier if I had been taking a proper shot of her rather than making her some minor detail in my big *"composition"*. I must admit she has a point. On another night I might have lingered for a chat. But her use of the conditional tense leaves me in no doubt I have missed the decisive moment. Catching *le moment décisif* was, as I now recall, the key factor in the best work of the great French photojournalist Henri Cartier Bresson. All I can manage is a vaguely apologetic Gallic shrug as I take my leave of the lady. I wonder what Henri would have done in the circumstances.

  Time was when travelling on my own I would have clutched at any opportunity for human contact. But on this trip I'm not looking for company. In fact, I would even like to be released from being with my own self. Detached from my normal identity, I could roam free like pure spirit. In fact, I am convinced that you can't even begin to travel properly unless you leave your old self at home. Surely, being someone else somewhere else is the secret of the true traveller?

  I end up doing a couple more night shots. A banner over the Baroque entrance of the *Hôtel de Ville* on *Place Foch* announces that Ajaccio was the first town in France to be liberated on 9 September 1943. Then, on my way home I can't resist shooting *Le Grand Café Napoléon*. RG, in a rare *jeu de mots*, all the more enjoyable for that, describes the décor as Second Empire and the clientele as *troisième âge*. Pretty good.

  Right now there is no clientele at all. The place is completely deserted. What grabs me are the rows of empty chairs and tables emblazoned with the imperial N. It's endless capital Ns in all directions reflected to infinity in large mirrors. It's a clear case of N to the nth. Ho, ho. I hastily scribble my own little witticism in my notebook. And so to bed.

Suddenly, I am shattered. Fortunately, it's only a few steps further along *Cours Napoléon* back to *Hôtel Kallisté*. I enter room 307 and accept the indifferent embrace of my solitude, thinking I might just as well be in outer space on the dark side of the moon as here in Corsica, so detached am I right now from everything that defines me. It's a curious sense of existential weightlessness, like being no-one nowhere. I'm still on day one and yet I feel I have travelled a million miles.

Friday 22 September

I awake not knowing where I am. The room is pitch black. Though with the shutters firmly shut that could mean anything. Is it still yesterday? Perhaps it's tomorrow already. Or could it simply be today? It feels like all three rolled together into one timeless, sleepless bundle. I switch on the light. It's only 1.30am

Now my mind whirrs into action, completely at the mercy of all those tedious in-the-middle-of-the-night doubts and anxieties that invariably start with something of no consequence and escalate from there.

Tonight's routine begins with a tiny niggling question. Should I take the 6.10am bus to Bastia airport or fork out 50 euros on a taxi? No matter that this great decision doesn't need to be made for several days yet. Like a petulant child it stamps its foot and demands an immediate answer. So I dutifully weigh up the pros and the cons, figure out the various angles, and come to no particular view on the matter.

Already the damage is done. My wide awake brain insists on reviewing every aspect of the itinerary I have planned for the next few days. Would I be better off with an extra day in Ajaccio and cut short my time in Calvi? What about the dodgy weather forecast for Sunday? If there's a seriously heavy storm heading for Corsica, as *Corse-Matin* informed me earlier, then maybe

I should cut my losses and jump on a ship from Calvi to Nice?

It occurs to me that the advantage of this is I won't need to agonise further over the Bastia airport bus versus the 50 euros outlay on a taxi. Once safely off the island and back on *le continent* I can take my time, return at leisure to London from Nice overland. Maybe take the train? Second class *couchette* shouldn't break the bank. That's how we used to travel. Pretty damn uncomfortable it was too. Never slept a wink.

But hold it. If there's a really big storm on the way then the ferry might not sail at all. Or if it does it could sink. In which case there's nothing left to worry about, except how long I can expect to survive in the Med at this time of year. Possibly all night.

The thought of shipwreck revives my original plan to fly home from Bastia. So now it's just a matter of deciding whether to take the 6.10am airport bus or fork out 50 euros on a taxi. I find myself back exactly where I started on the mental treadmill.

How ridiculous a waste of brain power is stuff like that? I recall the excellent advice of Lao Tzu, the ancient Chinese philosopher and founder of Taoism, on the art of travel: *"A good traveller has no fixed plans, and is not intent on arriving."* Nice thinking, Lao Tzu. But you've been dead two and half thousand years. Times have changed and so have travellers' expectations.

To your oriental wisdom I would humbly add a few thoughts of my own. A real traveller should not even think about home. Just keep on travelling until the journey reaches its own proper conclusion. I repeat my previous statement about not bringing yourself with you. Forget who you are and where you came from. Otherwise you might just as well have stayed at home.

I reflect on the roller coaster nature of happiness. Just a few hours ago I was on top of the world, up for whatever Corsica cared to throw at me. Now here I am unable to sleep, with a head full of confusing and depressing nonsense. I tell myself that unhappiness is transient too. I take a deep breath and count to ten.

So it's just a matter of nursing the trip through a bad patch. On no account let it stall. Man on the move must not lose momentum. That's the worst that can happen to a traveller. The slip from being a person with a purpose to someone just pointlessly somewhere he shouldn't be is a ghastly prospect. Must bring the journey back home intact, a well tied parcel, all bundled up in a neat package to be unwrapped and savoured whenever needed for future reference. There and back. Where I've been. The stuff of memories.

Ah, that's better already. Sleep comes but only lasts until my travel alarm wakes me. Its stifled beeping reaches my ears from deep within the camera bag. It is only 4.47am. What's going on? For a moment I'm completely disoriented. Am I supposed to be getting ready for the 6.10 bus to Bastia airport? No. Not that. I'm still in Ajaccio. Suddenly I recall setting the alarm for wake up at Gatwick, just in case I were to fall asleep in that big armchair and miss my flight. Oh dear. Too much planning, you see. Lao Tzu was right.

God, what a night. It's sheer relief to emerge at the other end, finally waking at 8am. After a shower I feel OK. Have a quick look at hotel breakfast room and decide to take my chances in town. Besides I don't like to eat first thing. I prefer to let my hunger grow. So I opt to walk it around the block a few times like a little dog until it starts to growl.

Off we go in the general direction of the market. First photo opportunity of the day is of serried ranks of cake tins, all bearing the likeness of a grumpy Napoleon, like a toy army consisting entirely of the general. How many battles would be fought if the commander-in-chief had to man the front line with clones of himself? Then I wonder how Napoleon would have felt being portrayed on a cake tin. Being used posthumously for product endorsement possibly a more bitter pill to swallow than defeat at Waterloo?

That reminds me, I must check the opening hours of the *Maison Bonaparte*, the house where the great man was born in 1769. I consult the map to get my bearings. But my little dog has started barking. Time for breakfast. As if by magic I find a café attached to a *boulangerie*. I order the *formule petit-déjeuner avec croissant* and then *baguette avec beurre et confiture* for good measure. Chirpy young waitress tells me that'll be a 2 euros *supplément*. Yes, dear. I think I can manage that. I drink my *café* black. Strong, acrid taste sets my nerves jangling as it clears the space behind the eyes. Day already hot and set fair. A lot of ground to cover.

First I scan today's *Corse-Matin*. The front page headline announces a story on page 3: *"Violence sur les personnes: rien d'alarmant en Corse."* Violence against persons, nothing alarming in Corsica? What can that mean? Well, according to the article, violent crimes in Corsica are up on last year. But allowing for seasonal adjustments such as a number of incidents associated with specific disturbances which can be disregarded for statistical purposes, then this year's figures are really not that bad, or so says Michel Delpuech, the Prefect for Corsica South. So basically it's good news really. Crime is rising and falling at the same time.

As for violence against property, that's another matter. In fact, it has become something of a Corsican speciality. Attacks on foreigners' second homes – and that includes the French – are an alarmingly common occurrence. Last month a whole spate of incidents occurred in Corsica all on the same evening, described in the local press as a *nuit bleue*. Can that be a visual reference to the blue lights of the police cars rushing to the scene? Anyway, these bombings of property even made it into the national press back home.

Simon Jenkins relayed the story in The Guardian of 30 August 2006:

"Villa owners arriving on the island of Corsica this summer had a rude shock. Many found their "second homes" blown to bits. The separatist Corsican National Liberation Front (FLNC) had broken a ceasefire declared last year after losing a referendum on more autonomy for the island. In recent weeks, bombings have risen from two a month to five a night. The

buildings are empty and usually new, and the nervous authorities are reluctant to condemn the mounting destruction."

As for the motives of the perpetrators, the story continues:

"Corsican nationalists complain that newcomers have driven up land prices tenfold in eight years. With local people ageing and the young escaping to mainland France, villages are becoming like the Var and Provence, half-deserted second-home economies. Corsican culture and language is disappearing as family and social bonds are broken. Island politics is torn between developers eager to attract the rich and nationalists demanding a 10-year qualification for anyone buying property. This tension is lurching into violence."

I have some sympathy for local frustrations about the second home phenomenon in places where ordinary folk now struggle to buy their first home as a result of richer outsiders purchasing real estate. With the mounting problem of homelessness it doesn't seem fair that some people should collect houses they don't rightly need thereby making life even more difficult for those unable to afford even one. But surely we already have too much violence in the world?

Let's get back to Napoleon Bonaparte. The past, however messy and blood-stained, is somehow far less troubling than the problems of the present. *Maison Bonaparte* opens its doors in a few minutes, and I want to get in ahead of the crowds. I get an idea of what is in store on *Place Foch* where a group of Swedish tourists has gathered to listen to their guide in front of an imposing statue of Napoleon.

By contrast to the marble Bonaparte in Bastia, this Ajaccio version shows the man in more statesmanlike mode. Once again he is in Roman gear but this time fully covered rather than flaunting the flesh. His expression is reflective and his general demeanour altogether more modest. One would guess a senator rather than emperor. But there are too many people in the way for more than a cursory glance and a couple of souvenir snaps.

The moment I step inside the birthplace of Napoleon Bonaparte I sense this is going to be different from the average museum. Here I am standing in the hall of the childhood home of a man feared and loathed by the British in his day just as in more recent times the likes of Adolf Hitler and Saddam Hussein.

Bringing *Boney* to book engaged the political will and military muscle of an entire generation. Bloody campaigns were fought all over Europe on land and sea. Thousands of men were killed or suffered horrific wounds. Fortifications were hastily erected along the south coast of England in full expectation of a French invasion by the *Grande Armée* under the command of this charismatic Corsican upstart with the leadership and martial renown of Alexander the Great.

There's no attempt in *Maison Bonaparte* to hype the reputation of the man born here on 15 August 1769 into the Buonaparte family and given the name *Napoleone*, also spelled *Nabolione* or *Nabulione* in the Corsican dialect. The ethnic origins of France's most powerful European leader since Louis XIV were thus

Italian rather than French. But the Napoleonic era was a short-lived affair. France's bid for imperial glory ended in tears with defeat at Waterloo. The country has since walked in the shadows, never again really to strut her stuff on the world stage as *une grande nation* with any great conviction.

Nor can Corsica wholeheartedly embrace the memory since the lasting legacy of Napoleon's meteoric rise to the top job in Paris brought no special perks to his native island. According to one view, he actually helped condemn Corsica to its present subordinate status as a couple of *départments* administered from Paris in quasi neo-colonial fashion. Nor did Napoleon exactly endear himself to his kinsmen even with kind words. Looking back at Corsica from his exile on St Helena he stated: *"M de Choisel once said that if Corsica could be pushed under the sea with a trident, it should be done. He was right. It is nothing but an excrescence."* That's pretty strong language.

As for special ties to his home town of Ajaccio, there is naturally pride in the huge achievements of their local boy. As previously noted, Napoleon did elevate Ajaccio to capital of Corsica, but that may have been done on the old principle of 'divide and rule' as a direct snub to Bastia. One last snippet, this gleaned from RG, is that Napoleon put Ajaccio fourth on the list of places where he would like to be buried. Fourth? What an insult, that's not even a podium place.

At this point, I must pause for breath and state that I haven't come here on some kind of Napoleonic mission to recite chapter and verse. But it's impossible to ignore the great man in Corsica; and some things are of genuine interest so I set them down. For example, it's worth mentioning that his mother Letizia doted on her little *Nabulio* (lovely pet name that) who spent the first nine years of his life in this patrician house in downtown Ajaccio before taking advantage of French scholarships to finish his schooling *sur le continent* first at the Brienne military academy then the more prestigious *École Militaire* in Paris.

The frenchifying of *Napoleone di Buonaparte* to *Napoléon Bonaparte* in 1793 marked his cultural and political transition from the small stage of Corsican issues to the great theatre of French ambitions.

I sense there was only one person in the world Napoleon Bonaparte respected alongside himself. His mum. She is referred to here on the text panels by her popular nickname *Madame Mère* which translates literally as *Mrs Mother*. This honorific title exudes a natural authority. This is borne out by a tribute from the great man himself: *"It is to my mother and to her good principles that I owe my fortune and everything of good that I have done."*

By contrast, Napoleon probably considered his dad *Carlo* a bit of a loser on account of his pro-British leanings. However, *Charles*, as he was posthumously Gallicised, passed away when *Nabulio* was still in his teens so this never became an issue. At a tender age Napoleon assumed his role as effective head of the family and he never looked back.

The actual room where Napoleon was born now functions more as a corridor. You could walk through it without pausing for a second glance. The story goes that *Madame Mère* went into labour in her sedan chair on her way home from the cathedral. The ancient conveyance is stored rather than displayed under the stairs near the exit as if it still gets an occasional outing.

Maison Bonaparte in the post-Napoleonic era was often rented out to British tourists like a holiday *gîte*. So a lot of memorabilia went missing. Still, there's plenty left. Large items of furniture couldn't be easily removed and some striking museum pieces have been brought here more recently from elsewhere. Among these are plaster death masks that look amazingly like François Mitterand while he was still alive. I always thought there was something funereal about Mitterand's face; and now I have it proved that he modelled his deadpan expression on Napoleon's death mask.

However, it's the idea of Napoleon the superstar, first mega celebrity of the modern era that I take away with me. He may have lost at Waterloo and ended his life in obscure exile on a remote island he regarded as yet another excrescence to be pushed under the sea. But the man is immortal. He simply will not die. He will never go away, and it's not all on account of his achievements on and off the battlefield but also down to his premeditated exploitation of image, the cult of a personality promoted through idealised portraits, iconic trappings of fashion, design and trademark poses.

Without even knowing who Napoleon really was or even what he did, we immediately recognise him as one of the all-time most famous people to have lived on

Planet Earth. Long after the transient supermodels and sportsmen of our era are dust and ashes, Napoleon will remain, still having movies made and books written about him, endorsing products from biscuits to brandy. And yes, having your face on a cake tin comes with the territory of the super celeb. No disrespect there, *Boney*. You are a brand, one hell of a global brand.

The N magic also worked in mysterious ways on Napoleon's enemies. Statues and busts of the defeated emperor were not just trophies of war to gloat over, but also prized possessions exuding a bizarre fascination to be venerated almost like sacred relics. For 75 years a tableau was exhibited at Madame Tussaud's waxworks in London depicting the scene of Napoleon on his deathbed. Wellington himself was a frequent visitor. Yes, even he fell under Napoleon's spell.

Wellington may have had the glory of victory and a long life as national hero feted with annual *Waterloo Banquets* in Apsley House. Meanwhile Napoleon has won the long-term battle for a permanent place in human remembrance. You don't get an equivalent cult of Wellington with a lively trade in *Wellingtonia*, now do you? Lesser mortals from Stalin and Hitler to Mussolini have borrowed every trick from Napoleon's book but have since fallen by the wayside. *Nabulio*, you are still the man. Shame you never got to cash in on any of those lucrative sponsorship deals.

Don't think I'm a closet Bonapartist with a secret wardrobe full of big hats, great coats and shiny boots. It was a good thing Napoleon's dream of world dominion ended at Waterloo. Otherwise, a French empire with dictatorial rather than democratic tendencies might have taken the place of the British early in the 19th century and laid the cultural and political foundations of our modern world. Can you imagine France letting go of colonies without a bloodier struggle than America's War of Independence? So many aspects of life would be different: the President of the USA massacring French instead of English. India and Australia playing *boules* instead of cricket. Now, that's a thought.

I stagger out into the sunshine of *rue Bonaparte* and make towards *Place de Gaulle*. It's almost noon and I slip into the cathedral for a few quiet non-Napoleonic moments because there's plenty more of the N brand on today's menu. A friendly *Madame* shuts the main door behind me with a large key. Clunk. Am I to be locked in over the lunch break along with a solitary pigeon flapping about in the dome above me? The trapped bird might be a symbol of something.

Before I can figure out what that might be, here comes *Madame* brandishing her clutch of keys to usher me out through a side door. *"Je vous souhaite…"* are her parting words. *"I wish you …"* Wish me what? I guess I can complete the sentence any way I want, filling in the blanks with *"a nice day"*, *"bon appétit"* or whatever I fancy. Now that's a nifty linguistic device. To deliver it correctly you must leave it hanging in the air, not finish it off as a completed phrase. *"Je vous souhaite…"* I make several attempts. It's not as easy as you think.

Apart from the name, *Place de Gaulle* has nothing to do with General Charles of that appellation. Pride of place goes once more to Napoleon here portrayed in a formidable equestrian statue. Yet again he is kitted out in Roman costume, but this time more in the style of an imperial conqueror with golden victory wreath on his head and bearing orb of empire in his right hand. Full of pomp and circumstance, he is flanked by the figures of his four brothers escorting him like outriders except they are on foot to reflect their lower status.

It's not great sculpture but there's a real drama to the composition. Napoleon and his brothers all point in the same direction like cowboys heading off into the sunset. As I try to get a good angle, not easy from ground level looking up, I discover the shady benches behind the plinth are the favourite haunt of Ajaccio's drinking fraternity. Napoleon has more brothers than he realises. At last I find the best shot is from the rear precisely in the middle in order to get all five figures in frame. So I shoot a couple of pics, right up the horse's arse as it were, and make my exit.

I am now following Ajaccio's prestige street, running straight as an arrow up a steepish hill. Above the ill-tempered hooting traffic hang garlands and oval-shaped medallions of Napoleon as if the Emperor is currently in town on a state visit. The thoroughfare itself is full of political and historic significance, starting down at *Place Foch* as *avenue du Premier Consul*, then morphing into *avenue de Paris*, *Cours Grandval* and *Cours*

Général Leclerc, the latter two prominent men among Napoleon's military commanders.

It seems the map of Ajaccio is well permeated with Napoleonic nomenclature. Mother *Letizia* has both a street and a square named after her. *Impératrice Eugénie* gets an avenue. Even Ajaccio's cinemas muscle in on the Napoleonic act with names like *Bonaparte, Empire, L'Aiglon* and *Laetitia*. I search in vain, however, for any small thing named after *Joséphine*.

But what's this? There's a *Rue Miss Campbell* off to the left next to a grand old pile sporting the faded name of *Cyrnos Palace*. I press my nose against the glass pane on the vestibule door. It's as trapped in time as an aspidistra but evidently with people living there.

That evening it takes a quick Google in a cyber café to discover Miss Campbell once owned a grand hotel in Ajaccio called the *Cyrnos Palace*. She also built Ajaccio's Anglican church at her own expense. This was in the second half of the 19th century when Victorian travellers added Ajaccio to their favourite winter haunts of Nice and Menton on the French Riviera. I can't find out much more on Miss Campbell than this but I imagine her as a formidable *grande dame* to be played in a lavish period costume movie by Dame Maggie Smith.

Google also comes up with an article in *L'Express*, the French weekly magazine, reviewing an exhibition on the history of tourism in Corsica. It seems those pioneering Brits were such popular visitors they were sorely missed in the early years of the 20th century. Indeed to such an extent that the locals coined a phrase in Corsican dialect *forsa scalaranu l'Inglese* as an optimistic expression of hope that the English would return and good times come round again.

Brits come back! What on earth would Napoleon Bonaparte have made of that? Anyway, Miss Campbell's church is now a dance studio, and her posh *Cyrnos Palace* is used for social housing. If I were a citizen of Ajaccio I'd put my name down for a council flat at the *Cyrnos* and never need or want to go on holiday again.

My stomach is now grumbling but it's learned over the years that meals are flexible feasts when I'm on the trail of something. Before I can even think about lunch there's one more hugely important Napoleonic monument to be ticked off. Already I see my target up ahead perched on the rocky outcrop of a hill rising above a park called *Jardins du Casone*.

On entering I see it's not so much a park as a massive parade ground with a barren sandy surface shimmering in the mid-day heat. It is deserted but for a young Russian couple in bike leathers who ask me to take their picture. I do so. Then they are gone.

So now it's just the two of us. Me down here, Napoleon Bonaparte up there on his stepped pyramid. I take a deep swig of tepid water, discard the empty plastic bottle and commence my ascent. A long staircase leads up past the roll call of Napoleon's many battles. But for battles read victories because the final one in the alphabetical list is absent. After Wagram there's no Waterloo to round things off. I note that

Moscow does figure even though that campaign ended with one of the most abject retreats of all time.

More interesting than the famous *victoires* is the inventory of Napoleon's civic achievements: *BANQUE DE FRANCE, CODE CIVIL, UNIVERSITÉ, LÉGION D'HONNEUR, COURS DES COMPTES, CONCORDAT, CONSEIL D'ÉTAT.* You can see why the French still have high regard for Napoleon as a nation builder. Curious that it took a Corsican to create institutions now regarded as quintessentially French. So along with his PR savvy and image promotion skills there was also a statesman of real substance.

His name is billed in big letters carved in stone as *NAPOLEON I.* The title seems strange. Yes, there were two other Napoleons in this short-lived imperial dynasty so that does make him the first of three. But it strikes me as superfluous to put a numeral after the name of the one and only Napoleon that matters. Like a posthumous demotion to line him up with others who shared his name, rather like calling William the Conqueror, William I. Not the same thing at all.

I pause to study the statue. This is my fourth sculptural encounter with Napoleon Bonaparte after the one in Bastia and the two I've just seen in downtown Ajaccio. This one is a replica of the famous original adorning his burial place at *Les Invalide*s in Paris and it feels very much like Napoleon at the end of his glittering, blood-soaked career, poised to take leave of this petty life. So he's looking middle-aged and with a decent paunch. His brooding look is directed down below to the world he is leaving behind as well as up to the warriors' retirement home in the heavens above.

I'm now at the top of the staircase. Too close to the statue on top of its stepped pyramid to get a decent view. But I can make out the familiar outline of the lone figure standing on his own two booted legs, slightly slouched as if that big coat was too heavy for him. He's wearing his characteristic huge hat that must have been hard to hold on to in a strong wind. I'm as close as you are supposed to get but something drives me on.

I walk round the back of the statue safely out of sight and commence the final ascent scrambling up half a dozen huge tiers of stone that taper upwards to the summit. I see I am not the first to do this because the cannon balls heaped up behind Napoleon like so many knobs of horse manure have been autographed by previous visitors. Just one more step and I'll be right up there alongside the great Napoleon. I have no head for heights but I'm really curious to see what his view looks like. I want to share, albeit for a moment or two, his dizzying perspective on the world.

What a lonely sight it is. I find myself humming *The Fool on the Hill* not in a mocking manner, but more to fill the awful emptiness of this one man Valhalla. Here stands Napoleon Bonaparte without his brothers, *Madame Mère* or *Joséphine*. The closer to the Gods, so it seems, the fewer humans there are. Just a pair of stone eagles survey the *Jardins du Casone* down below, a deadly expanse of nothingness, a vacant parade ground with no *Grande Armée* to be drilled, to shout hurrah, *vive l'empereur*, toss hats in the air and then march off to death or glory.

The faithful soldiers are palpable by their absence. I can understand why that Chinese emperor wanted to be buried with his terracotta warriors as companions. Before I leave Napoleon to contemplate eternity it's only fair he should have the last word. The following quote fits the bill. *"Glory is fleeting but obscurity is forever."* There speaks a man with no illusions about anything. So I guess he would have no quarrel with the ultimate outcome. After all, his flame is still burning bright two centuries later.

For my part I would far prefer to be down in the town with the drunks gulping cheap red wine in the shadow of the horse's arse on *Place de Gaulle* than up here communing with the implacable gods of destiny and war. Give me obscurity any day. With that parting shot, thoughts turn to lunch.

I trudge back down the hill, noting *Hôtel Albion* and wondering if that name would be possible on mainland France without a *perfide* by way of a prefix. Somewhere off to my left in the next fold of the hillside are *Les Jardins de l'Empereur*. But I'm feeling overdosed on Napoleon so I let gravity lead me down *rue Miss Campbell* and on to the sea where I soon find what I'm after at *Plage St François*.

It's a simple restaurant with a few tables outside in the shade of an awning under the trees. Only one or two other customers, so it's not too crowded. Paper tablecloths are a good sign. They usually mean less fuss and lower prices. There's also a pizza menu just in case I don't fancy any of the *plats du jour* plus a teasing view in the background of the sparkling blue waters of the Bay of Ajaccio. All I need for total bliss, as I wriggle hot feet out of shoes and flex my toes in the fresh air, is the magical sound of Charles Trenet singing *La Mer*.

The haunting melody and opening lines of this passionate love song to the sea, so typically French in every way, come back to me.

"*La mer
Qu'on voit danser
Le long des golfes clairs…*"

It may be more widely known in its blander English version *Beyond the Sea*, recorded many times by star crooners Bing Crosby, Bobby Darin, Dean Martin, Frank Sinatra, Barbara Streisand and Sarah Vaughan. But the original French has a more mysterious, poetic, virtually untranslatable quality. I only need to shut my eyes to be transported back half a century to a French beach somewhere in Normandy or Brittany. I can almost see the sun glinting off the blue waves.

Against my better judgement I order a *pichet* of dry *vin blanc* to drink alongside the ice cold mineral water. Alcohol at lunchtime on a hot day invariably makes for a heavy afternoon and I still have more miles ahead on the Napoleonic heritage trail. I'm so happy with the day thus far it seems only right to mark the occasion. The crisp white wine is nothing special but really hits the spot. On an empty stomach I am instantly mellow. By the third sip I am already up to cruising altitude. Time to ease back on the throttle and take in the view. Life as ever looks pretty good through the bottom of a wine glass.

When my *gratin de poisson au spaghetti* arrives I feel the still life scene of my luncheon table is sufficiently memorable to deserve a souvenir snap. Charles Trenet, meanwhile, continues to croon *La Mer* on an endless loop though getting softer all the time until the magic melody fades away like a morning mist in the sunshine. Gently I ease back into the real world. Ah, they don't write songs like that any more.

Right after lunch I witness a cameo performance on the beach worthy of Jacques Tati with soundtrack by Charles Trenet. An elderly man is instructing his wife in the art of holiday snaps. I watch him explaining how to frame the shot and press the button. Then he takes up his position standing in the sea like the *jeune sportif* he was many years ago. Meanwhile, I record the moment. I shall call my picture *The Photography Lesson, Plage St François*. Very satisfying.

It's pretty hard going with even a modest *pichet* of white wine in the tank. So a brief rest in the cathedral dedicated to the Assumption of the Blessed Virgin Mary, now re-opened after the lunch break, provides a welcome breather. A marble plaque by the entrance shows how important this church was to Napoleon. It bears a quotation supposed to be the words spoken by him as he lay dying on St Helena.

"If they forbid my corpse, as they have forbidden my body, a small piece of land in which to be laid, I desire to be buried with my ancestors in Ajaccio cathedral in Corsica".

So how does that square with RG's comment that Ajaccio ranked only fourth on Napoleon's burial wish list? But it's more than likely that Napoleon made various and varying comments on the subject of his last resting place, on which matter he had ample time to ponder and change his mind.

Napoleon may not have been buried in Ajaccio Cathedral but he was certainly baptised here on 21 July 1771. The marble font used on that occasion consists of a plain basin with a bronze cover added later bearing the Latin inscription *HEIC BAPTISATUS IMPERATOR MAGNUS* which translates word for word as *GREAT EMPEROR BAPTISED HERE*. Perhaps it was deemed superfluous to mention the name of the great emperor in question.

It was also here on 15 August 1769 during the mass of the Assumption to celebrate the first year of Corsica's attachment to France, that Napoleon's mother Letizia felt the birth pangs heralding the arrival of little *Nabulio*. This ties in nicely with the story that *Madame Mère* went into labour in the sedan chair on her way home from the cathedral. Before leaving the church I look about for the trapped pigeon but there is no sign of its presence, nor of *Madame* with her bunch of keys and enigmatic *"Je vous souhaite…"*

My next and final Napoleonic port of call is the Bonaparte family mausoleum, formerly housed in the cathedral, but subsequently transferred during the Second Empire to the *Chapelle Impériale* in the *Palais Fesch*. But since the port is close at hand I decide to check that out first.

As in Bastia the fishing part has been squeezed to make room for yet another *port de plaisance*. I feel the same death in the soul at the sight of all those mass produced fibreglass boats neatly lined up on their floating parking lot. True a small area is designated as *port de pêche*. I dutifully snap a brightly painted wooden fishing boat which looks as if it has been artfully placed on a pedestal for that very purpose. So even as I click away I have the unpleasant sensation I'm helping to perpetuate a cosy myth that the old is co-existing nicely on equal terms with the new.

However, I am glad to see the big vessels of the rival shipping companies SNCM and Corsica Ferries that link the island with *le continent*. I'm reminded of my previous speculation on possible escape routes ahead of the approaching storm. Yet the sky remains deep blue and the sea not unduly choppy, though according to the latest weather forecast the outlook is still distinctly unsettled. But while things are going well, making hay in the sun shine seems the best policy. Briefly I consider taking a boat trip to the nearby *Îles Sanguinaires*, but the name *Bloody Islands* puts me off.

The *Chapelle Impériale* forms part of what is now the *Musée Fesch* and I must first obtain an entry ticket from the museum. The purchase of this simple *billet* goes down as one of life's great milestones. For it is here and now that I obtain my very first senior citizen's concession. I'm not sure how it comes about but the friendly cashier, a man of my own generation, enquires diplomatically if I might qualify.

When I reply *"Well, almost…"* he asks *"When?"* To which I then reply *"In a month."* At this he waves a hand in the air as if to say *"Is that all? We aren't the sort of people to quibble about a month here or there."* So I start to reap the benefits of being sixty a full two months ahead of schedule. Yes, I have lied about my age in the hope of a small saving. That will be a nice pre-senior moment to remember.

I cross an enormous sun-baked courtyard past a bronze statue of Cardinal Fesch. I'll have more to say about him in a moment. But first I enter the cool, gloomy interior of the *Chapelle Impériale*. The main item of interest lies down in the crypt where various members of the Bonaparte clan are laid to rest.

In adjoining vaults lie Napoleon's parents. His mother is given her full maiden name Maria-Letizia Ramolino. The sensitive issue whether to call his father *Carlo* as per the original Italian version of his name or *Charles* as in the later French version, has been cleverly circumvented by the use of the Latin *Carolus*. In fact, there was the potential for a major political rift between Bonaparte *père*, who supported the short-lived Anglo-Corsican alliance and Bonaparte *fils* who upheld the new union with France. That father and son never fell out irrevocably is almost certainly entirely due to the early demise of *Carlo/Charles/Carolus*.

With that I reckon I've had my fill of Napoleon Bonaparte & family. Well, almost. It turns out that Cardinal Fesch, whose statue I now inspect, complete with pigeon perched ominously on his bronze head, was Napoleon's uncle. So out comes camera followed by notebook to record my impressions. Luckily RG is on hand to inform me that this influential cleric used his lucrative status as Bishop of Lyon to 'invest' in a remarkable collection of paintings looted by the French army on its rampages through Europe. These spoils of war are now housed in the *Musée Fesch*.

I gaze up at the angelic face of Cardinal Fesch. His pious expression and wide open upturned eyes say most eloquently that butter wouldn't melt in his mouth. His right hand placed symbolically on his heart dares the onlooker to find any wrong in him. It's almost as if he's protesting his innocence. Who, me?

Following RG's directions I head for level 3 to see Botticelli's 'exquisite' *Virgin and Child* and Titian's 'smouldering' *Man with a Glove*. After a fruitless quarter of an hour I have to ask a custodian who tells me that these works are in fact located on level 1. And so they are. Here I also discover Veronese's *Leda and the Swan*, 'an uncompromising erotic work for its time'. You're right enough there, RG. This picture is high octane stuff, giving a whole new meaning to 'bird lover'.

Sadly Titian's *Man with Glove* is temporarily out on loan. So with a blank wall to admire instead of *L'Homme au Gant*, my mind goes off down memory lane. It's all to do with the word *gant*. I recall vaguely at first, then with embarrassing clarity the absolute howler I made in Paris one mid-winter night many years ago.

I was collecting my key from the *Madame* who presided over the bar of a small Left Bank hotel. A clutch of regulars were sipping steaming glasses of *grog* and making small talk about how bitterly cold it was. Seizing the opportunity to make a harmless remark of my own about the weather I waited for a lull in the conversation. *"Yes, it's bloody freezing and to cap it all I've just lost my gloves"* is what I think I said to the assembled company in my best schoolboy French.

When the uncontrolled hoots of derisive laughter finally abated several minutes later – it seemed much longer at the time – I learned for my future instruction, just in case the knowledge would ever come in handy, ho ho ho, that *perdre ses gants* is a colloquial French term meaning to lose one's virginity. More hoots of laughter at this point. I hope I had the good grace to laugh along though I'm not sure I did. I offer this anecdote as a testimonial to the high price I've paid for whatever prowess in French I may have acquired over the years.

After this awkward memory I turn a corner and find myself staring at Bellini's *Virgin and Child*. This famous canvas doesn't get a mention by RG. Perhaps he isn't a Bellini man. Now a Bellini is a cocktail of peach juice and champagne or *spumante* invented at the legendary *Harry's Bar* in Venice. I recall a pleasurable drinking session there on another cold winter day with the high tide pushing the swollen Adriatic across the paving stones of St Mark's Square. But that would be a digression too far.

I head back to *Hôtel Kallisté* for a quick breather. I reflect again what a neat little establishment it is. They even provide an internet facility for guests. So it's a good moment to check my emails, weather forecast and so on. I'm logging out when something strikes me about the wallpaper on the start screen.

If I'm not mistaken it's the *Azzurri* those heroic men in blue kissing the World Cup after their famous victory over France in Berlin. Maybe there are some Italian supporters among the staff here? I ask the guy on the reception desk. He gives a non-committal shrug saying *"Well not really…"* Then the penny drops. *"So it's to piss off your French guests?"* A broad smile and a quick nod of the head tells me the Corsica-France relationship must be roughly on a par with Scotland-England.

How Corsica must have erupted when French captain Zinedine Zidane got himself sent off right at the end of the final by head-butting Italian defender Marco Materazzi in the chest.

Room 307 admits me back into its monastic calm and simplicity. A late afternoon shower has an amazing effect. I'm tingling all over. Lying on my back, I reflect that the Corsican trip has got off to a great start. The stress of the journey, the sheer hassle of getting myself from home to here, it's all been worth it. No, RLS, I haven't changed my mind. Arriving somewhere like this is far better than to travel hopefully.

The hotel tariff posted on the door in time-honoured fashion catches my eye. I discover that the rate I obtained by booking via the internet is cheaper than what I would have paid as a walk-in guest. That's pleasing as is the prospect of settling my own account.

I recall a comment by Michael Winner in one of his famously outspoken hotel and restaurant reviews in *The Sunday Times* to the effect that you can't trust a travel writer who doesn't pay his own bill. Yes, Michael, I can now agree. You're absolutely right. Not that you can necessarily trust a travel writer who does pay his own bill either. This thought comes as I now remember an experience on Madeira when I happened to walk into the wreckage of a very posh hotel that had just received a full artillery barrage from an extremely disgruntled Michael Winner.

I can't recall the precise details but the writer's brief stay at the highly rated Reid's Hotel had been an unmitigated disaster, at least according to MW whose article consisted of a litany of failings and mishaps rather like the horror stories tourists tell to convince you what a perfectly rotten time they've had.

Anyway, Reid's Hotel was ruthlessly rubbished by MW almost as an act of personal revenge. It was simply awful, readers of *The Sunday Times* were asked to believe. I entered the still smoking ruins to be greeted by a shell-shocked manager. His confusion at my presence in his hotel was understandable. Michael Winner's piece had only just appeared and here was I calmly checking in with a firm commission from the very same newspaper to write my own travel story.

The hotel manager was at pains to push the boat out and extend the warmest of welcomes. He apologised that his best room the *Winston Churchill Suite* was sadly unavailable on account of refurbishment but was pleased to offer us the next best thing. Over lunch the next day, he sounded me out on the nature of my mission. Was this the newspaper's way of making amends for Winner demolition job on Reid's?

"*Good lord, no.*" I heard myself replying. "*Michael Winner is a rule unto himself. Some places can do no wrong. Others can do no right. There's not much in between. It's the luck of the draw. Readers enjoy his rudeness. It's all part of the fun.*" Looking at his pained expression, I could tell it hadn't been much fun for Reid's Hotel.

My own story duly appeared in *The Sunday Times*. Its main theme was the various tropical gardens of Madeira, one of which happened to be the hotel's own garden. So Reid's ended up with a nice bit of publicity to compensate for the mauling by MW. An ingenious sub at the newspaper entitled my article SCENTS AND SENSIBILITIES. I felt that made me appear rather twee. I guess I deserved it. It was after all a typically well-mannered piece: in short, a regular pansy, if I may continue the floral theme.

Thoughts now turn to dinner. I mull over the possibilities while sipping a *pastis* at *Le Grand Café Napoléon*. Now in travel writer speak a café terrace is invariably a place to watch the world go by. Well that might be true if you've nothing better to do with yourself. But right now my thoughts are buzzing as the *pastis* enters the bloodstream.

Memories of *The Sunday Times* continue to haunt me. A fellow travel writer once recommended I should try my hand at submitting stories for the travel section's *Confessions of a Tourist* series. These little anecdotes are traveller's tales with an erotic twist, and they don't have to be entirely authentic, or so my confidant advised with a nod and a wink, letting slip that he often laced his confessions with a dose of fabrication. Trick is he said to write them as cameo sexual fantasies. Well, I didn't go for that at the time, but now I'm thinking what fun it would be to file my very own racy *Confessions of a Tourist* from Corsica, perhaps under an assumed name, and see if I have any luck with that.

But where does one have an erotic encounter in Ajaccio? RG is uncharacteristically silent on the subject. Then I remember that sexy thronged lady at the *Don Quichotte*. Yes, she'll do nicely. I'll devise some titillating tale involving her. At any rate, the venue for dinner is decided. It's back to the *Don Qichotte* for a three course *formule* and some material for my confessions.

Minutes later I am sitting at what I now regard as my table with a grandstand view of the bar and the lady doing her stuff under the Che Guevara picture. Yes, she is enticingly thronged as per yesterday evening. I take out my notebook and wait on inspiration. Nothing comes so I doodle with possible punning titles for my story: *Going for a Thong* is pretty good but then so is *There's a Thong in my Heart*.

I get no further with this except for the notion that my approaches might possibly get me into deep trouble with the lady's brother who then threatens a full scale *vendetta à la corse*, this causing me to panic and do a runner leaving my bill unpaid, making me guilty of the crime of *grivèlerie*. Amazing isn't it that the French have a special word for doing a bunk in a restaurant?

I once read a true story in a French newspaper of a hapless *griveleur* in a Nice restaurant who received summary justice from two irate waiters. They bundled the penniless customer onto the street, having stripped him of every shred of clothing. So don't count on doing the washing up in France to pay the bill.

So here am I scuttling through the alleyways by the port being pursued by an angry Corsican intent on an honour killing. I race round a blind corner and fall into the arms of that girl I'd inadvertently snapped the previous evening at *L'IDÉAL*. She whisks me away into her *bijou* apartment and the rest is …. .

No. None of this is remotely likely. It reeks of spoof from start to finish. Meanwhile, the waiter wants to take my order. I go for the *steak frites* and a decent red: the *Clos Colombu*. Perhaps a few swigs from *la dive bouteille* will do the trick. For the 'holy bottle' was the cure for everything according to François Rabelais author of *Gargantua* and *Pantagruel*.

But the wine is no help at all. In vain I try to find amusing ways of describing the cheeky red thong peeping over the waistband of her washed denim jeans. I might as well describe my own boxer shorts from Turnbull & Asser in Jermyn Street. Actually, I'm not even sure the pair I'm wearing isn't from Marks & Spencer. My point is the spontaneity has gone out of it. This isn't remotely fun or funny. It's certainly no longer erotic. I feel no better than a dirty old man.

Now I can't even look at the lady in case she catches my eye and reads my purpose. So I give up on trying to write a *Confessions of a Tourist*. It's no use at all, and it's ruining my dinner. I hardly notice the steak grilled *saignant* just as I like it. I close my notebook with a sigh of resignation.

So I haven't even got what it takes to cook up a simple traveller's tale. What's the problem? It might well be the drudge of writing to order. Producing something false and artificial even for such a worthy cause as a handful of silver suddenly seems if not entirely wrong then not quite right either.

Something now occurs to me with regard to Dr Johnson's dictum: *"No man but a blockhead wrote for any reason except money."* Quite possibly the exact opposite may be equally true. So let me say it loud and clear: *"No man but a blockhead wrote for reason of money."*

For unless writing comes from the heart or soul, it will perforce bear the taint of having been done for material gain rather than for its own true sake. That doesn't mean to say all professional writing is bad. It's just you can never be sure where you stand with a writer under contract to produce a quota of wordage.

But I'm not even convincing myself. So before I tie myself in knots let me extricate myself by saying as far as I'm personally concerned right now with a half bottle of *Clos Colombu* under my belt that I feel totally turned off formulaic hackery in any shape or form. Or at least until the next commission.

This realisation coincides with a passionate Corsican song delivered by a lady outside on the terrace. I can't begin to understand the words but they resonate in a *fado*-esque lament just like you hear in Lisbon. Next up is a young man howling to *la luna* as they do in Naples with an overdose of mandolins. Both singers in their different way leave me purring.

Once again I am at peace. Even the Brummie at the next table with his pizza and double helping of chips washed down with Coca Cola and tiresome tales of lost luggage cannot get to me. Perhaps he will win the heart of the red-thonged beauty and publish his own *Confessions of a Tourist*. As for me, it's goodbye to all that. After leaving the restaurant, the music seems to follow me up the street. My evening at *Don Quichotte* ends after all on a relative high.

I make a brief stroll through the old town. Then slowly back to the hotel. Early start tomorrow. I'm catching the morning train to Calvi. Feels strange to be saying farewell to Ajaccio already. Though it will be nice to step out into the Corsica that awaits beyond the long shadow of Napoleon Bonaparte.

The TV perched high up on a wall bracket in one corner of room 307 eyes me like a vulture from a branch. I make the mistake of turning it on. Lawrence Durrell once described living with a TV set as just like having a sick child in the house. I would not disagree. Instead of falling asleep I'm kept awake for half an hour watching the surreal spectacle of Hercule Poirot going through his paces dubbed into his native tongue of French. It all sounds far too natural, and there's no fun in a hammy French accent, *mon ami*, if you are actually speaking French. Or is there? On the other hand, I do get some big laughs from the stuffy Englishy tones of *Capitaine 'Astings* and *Inspecteur Yapp*.

Saturday 23 September

Wide awake in the wee small hours. Seems I have been wrestling with my 5 foot monster bolster pillow as desperately as that great statue in the Vatican Museum of Laocoon struggling with the serpent. Only with me and the bolster it's a less elegant contest than that carved by the ancient Greek sculptor.

Exhausted as I am, sleep simply won't come. I try to lull myself back into the land of nod by recalling some *chansons* by Juliette Gréco. I think I'm halfway through *Embrasse-Moi* when finally I drift off.

Alarm wakes me at 7. Having settled my bill the night before, all I have to do is drop key in letter box and slip away unobtrusively. Happy as I am in general with my time at *Hôtel Kallisté* I have no regrets about leaving room 307 where I've spent two restless nights.

Ajaccio is waking up. Even through my shuttered window the lovely aroma of freshly baked *croissants* comes wafting up. Down at street level, however, other smells hit the nostrils. The day's first dog poos have been deposited. The idea of breakfast at a pavement *café* loses its appeal. I press on to the station.

The *Buffet de la Gare* is not bad but the factory-baked *mini-baguettes* that come with the *formule petit-déjeuner* have a fatigued cardboardy texture. The *café au lait*, however, is just fine. It's also a great place to pass the time by the platform of the empty station. Even though the first stage of my journey to Calvi will once again be by rail replacement bus it's comforting to see the iron tracks stretching out purposefully into the distance. No bus garage can rival that.

This morning's *Corse-Matin* offers meagre fare. It looks like a load of press releases have been served up as front page news. Passenger numbers are reportedly well up on *Le Tramway de la Balagne*, and the railway engineering works proceed more or less on schedule – though sadly not fast enough for the purpose of today's journey. Air travellers to Corsica are showing a healthy increase but strangely enough visitor nights are down. There's a wistful passport-style picture of a tourism official who confirms this mysterious fact.

I discover something sinister buried away on an inside page. On Thursday night in Ajaccio, a bar called the *Billard Académie* was blown to bits. This resulted in light injuries to the young son of the owner and left the place a total wreck. The *patron* who had recently taken over the establishment was a Moroccan. He had been living in the area for ten years and got on well with everyone, or so he thought. There were no warnings and no threats. So the newspaper concludes rather disingenuously that it will be difficult to uncover the true motive for the attack.

Surely there's a small clue in the ethnic origin of the new owner? Wasn't that paintball attack on a café in Bastia aimed at North Africans? Perhaps the message is it may be OK for a Moroccan to work in a place like the *Billard Académie*. Though maybe he had better not get too big for his boots and aspire to ownership.

But let me not jump to conclusions and prejudice the enquiry. Suffice it to say for now that the victim, whose name is not published in the article, makes it thoroughly clear in a public statement, presumably for the benefit of those who may be interested, that he has no intention of rebuilding and starting again with the *Billard Académie*. He's had enough. He fears he could be bombed again at any time. End of story. As for the police investigation, I would suggest that finding motive may be far easier than identifying perpetrators.

So my lovely time in Ajaccio ends on a sour note, but I can leave that behind me. That's the good thing about travel. You can peer at or even prod the nasties lurking under the stones in other people's gardens, then move on serenely to the next place as if it were all a story or a dream.

Right on cue here is the rail replacement bus to take me away. At 8.53am we depart for Ponte-Leccia. On the way out of town we drive parallel to the railway line. Soon we are out in the country and reprise the long distance road-rail tango that so distracted me on the way in. Only this time we stop in more villages.

As we get further up into the hills a group of British walkers climbs aboard. Their youthful leader has www.exodus.co.uk printed on his T-shirt. They seem a jolly lot and fill the bus with cheery chat ahead of a strenuous trek in the mountains, if their gear is anything to go by. They alight a few miles further along the way.

After they've gone the bus suddenly feels empty. But Corsica seems more Corsican without them.

I'm sure the walkers will be getting a much better view of the mountain landscapes than me peering through the bus window at fleeting vistas of rocky crags, alpine pastures, isolated farmsteads, ruined stone buildings and herds of cows. Look, there's a dead one over there, right in the middle of a meadow, all on its own, the other cows keeping a respectful distance. I wonder how cows react to death. They must be aware that something has happened, isn't quite the same with one of their own.

At Ponte-Leccia we transfer from bus to train for the ride to Calvi. It's much busier now with plenty of folk milling about on the platform. When the short two carriage train pulls in I make a quick calculation which side I want to sit so as to be out of the sun and have a sea view for when we hit the coast. So I grab a seat on the right a couple of rows behind the driver. Only thing is, no sooner am I ensconced, than the driver scuttles off to the other end of the train leaving me well and truly scuttled. That means I'll be on the sunny side away from the sea at the back of the train. *Merde!*

By now all seats are occupied so I have no choice but stay put. Seasoned railway travellers may well smile at my inexperience in not checking which way the train would be heading. Elementary stuff surely. I reflect on my missed photo opportunity at this station a couple of days ago, So that makes it 2-0 to Ponte-Leccia. I'm playing away of course, as if that's any excuse.

At the last moment an olive-skinned young woman takes the seat next to me. Her efforts to place her large suitcase in the overhead rack are thwarted by a bossy Dutch or Belgian girl tourist who tells her *"c'est trop dangereux"*. She's right of course and there is even a notice stating that *Les Chemins de Fer Corses* take no responsibility for any accidents caused by luggage falling on heads of passengers. Looking up I see that my own small suitcase might well fall on my head. I don't want to appear unduly cautious so I leave it where it is.

The train transports us on through a parched, deserted landscape rather like southern California. Gazing idly out of the window, I soon reconcile myself to being on the wrong side of the train. Something alerts me that we are approaching the coast. When at last I catch a distant sight of the sea, a bright blue smudge on the horizon, I greet it with a half-suppressed gasp and all the surprised excitement of the small child on summer holiday I was many years ago.

We stop at L'Île Rousse, a popular beach resort where many people get off. I seize my chance and grab a vacant seat on the other side of the carriage. Now I'll have the sea views for the half hour ride along the coast to Calvi. What's more, I'm out of the burning sun and much happier with my back to the engine. For some inexplicable reason I do prefer to look back at what I'm leaving behind rather than ahead to what's coming.

Is travelling backwards significant? I recall some recent research I'd done ahead of a trip to New Zealand that has yet to happen. According to a serious academic article by Katharine Cox, Nancy G. Tayles and Hallie R. Buckley in *Current Anthropology*, the Maori time concept is fundamentally different from that of the West: *"While Westerners see time as stretching from the past behind to the future in front, Maori see the past in front of them and the future, which cannot be known, as stretching behind them."*

The idea is not as wayward as it might seem. Looking forward to what has gone before, as if it lies ahead, strikes me as a wonderful concept. Our shared human past dangles in front of us like a spider's abdomen from which the thread for our future web slowly unwinds. I find that strangely reassuring. The past continuous exists in the present tense. It makes us what we are. In short, the Maori View turns our logical future-oriented thinking firmly on its head.

So how do modern Maoris cope with today's obsession for projections and scenarios for what the world will be like in 10, 50, 100 years time? I remember on a trip to Japan I was acutely aware of being in a country where the future is being forged at least in terms of technology. I thought what fun it was if only for a short moment to sit next to the driver of the runaway train and watch tomorrow's world approach at breakneck speed. Like doing a white knuckle ride in a high-tech theme park.

Here in Corsica, rumbling along in the venerable rolling stock of *Les Chemins de Fer Corses* the Maori View comes naturally. The locals have a lovely name for their rattling old train. It's called the *micheline* in French and *trinighellu* or 'little train' in Corsican. But why *micheline*?

Well, the *Michelin Tyre Company* once designed and equipped rail cars. Now wouldn't it be great if the jovial fat figure of *Monsieur Michelin* better known as *Bibendum* could be put on the roof of the *trinighellu* like they do on long distance trucks?

As we leave L'Île Rousse there are great views of sandy beaches. Tourists stop what they are doing to wave us on our way, as if in slow motion, or snap the *micheline* as it crawls past. One photographer in safari outfit looks kitted out for a part as *Indiana Jones*. Altogether there's something pleasantly dated about the scene, like straying into a colour version of Jacques Tati's 1953 film classic *Monsieur Hulot's Holiday*, that glorious benchmark of a bygone era, beside which all other seaside experiences pale into insignificance. I can imagine Maori audiences lapping up *Les Vacances de Monsieur Hulot* for its nostalgic, unashamedly backward-looking take on summer holidays. I too am right in my element, enjoying this much more than expected.

A reminder of our more troubled times comes at Algajola where a ruined seaside villa with roof caved in has apparently been left to rot. Could this be the work of Corsican separatists on a foreigner's holiday home? There's no sign of a fire, just a mass of rubble.

Meanwhile, more passengers board the train. Now seated next to me is a lady a bit on the stout side, while her frail, elderly husband strap hangs precariously, there being no strap to hang on to, as the old *micheline* wobbles along the track. She gives some of the young folk a reproachful look for not offering him a seat. But perhaps they reckon she looks in pretty good nick herself and should be the first to do the honours.

Soon we are approaching Calvi: gorgeous views across a crescent bay of white sand and turquoise water towards the port huddled beneath a lofty citadel. It's the stuff picture postcards and panoramic posters are made of. I even take a photo of the *bella vista* from the moving train then kick myself for behaving like a tourist. Of course the shot will be useless. On the other hand, I'm not unhappy to be carrying on just like everyone else.

Before leaving the station there's a rare chance to play trains. Some of the old red and gold carriages are parked at the platform opposite. I hop over the tracks for a closer look. The doors are open so I slip inside. It really feels like the old *S-Bahn* in Berlin circa 1965 just as I'd noted back in Casamozza.

There's something about these ancient wagons that has me captivated. The rigid lines of the seats are hardly in tune with today's ideas of ergonomic comfort. So too the driver's cabin with its bewildering array of metal knobs, wheels and switches which would be more at home in an old steam locomotive.

I shoot a few pics then hurry back to my suitcase standing all alone on the station platform. Although there won't be another train for a couple of hours there is someone at the ticket office to tell me that the red and gold carriages are sixty years old or so. That makes them very much of my generation.

I walk the couple of hundred yards to the *Grand Hotel*. I hadn't wanted to go this upmarket but the

Grand was the easiest place in town to book via email and internet. Though when I queried the pricey room rate of 80 euros (including breakfast) and asked if the price quoted for a double could be reduced for single occupancy, I was promptly given a more expensive superior room with partial sea view at 84 euros. Seeing the way things were going I decided not to request any further concessions just in case they upgraded me to an executive suite with the appropriate tariff.

I note a numerical neatness in the nifty reversal of digits in the room rate from the 48 euros I paid in Ajaccio to 84 euros here in Calvi. There's another wee numerical surprise when the receptionist hands me the key to room 307. Room 307! That's exactly what I had in Ajaccio. I can't recall ever having the same room number at two successive hotels. It feels like a secret mathematical game directing my destiny. Someone or something else is pulling my strings.

In response to my enquiry about the weather the receptionist tells me today will be fine but looking ahead she warns of a big storm on the way. I revive my fallback plan of an escape route by ferry from Calvi to Nice, thereby saving myself the grim prospect of two wet days on a storm lashed Corsica. There should be a sailing tomorrow afternoon so that would mean cutting my stay at the *Grand* to just one night.

I explain the situation as best I can. The lady ventures the opinion that Corsica in the rain is not a jolly prospect. *"So would it be OK to make an early departure even though I've booked for two nights?"* She is really helpful.

As long as I inform her of my decision by this evening, then she'll *"arranger les choses"*.

Immediately, I wish I hadn't asked, and that she hadn't been so amenable. For now instead of settling in for a couple of nights in Calvi I've landed myself with a load of boring travel arrangements to make. Yes, Lao Tzu, I shouldn't be making plans. I might just as well not be in Calvi for all the good it is doing me.

Room 307 is nice enough, rather posh in fact, and there's even a distant sea view over the rooftops. But it all feels so transient if I am really going to leave tomorrow. I draw a deep breath and tell myself that nothing has changed, no decision made, so I should chill out and let things happen. No harm in checking the ferries though and then take it from there.

Meanwhile, let's have a look at Calvi. By contrast to Ajaccio, a real town with just a small strip of beach hardly big enough to qualify it as a resort, Calvi has *vacances* and *tourisme* writ large all over it. Holidaymakers in shorts and Hawaiian shirts stroll through narrow sun-dappled streets without any apparent purpose the way only *vacanciers* can manage.

As I approach the Citadel I enquire of an elderly couple who are speaking what I think is Swiss German if there's a tourist office in the old town. Turns out they are real Germans albeit from Waldshut just over the border from Switzerland, so I guess the accent leaks over by osmosis. They are friendly but they can't help since they've only just arrived themselves.

Ferries and tourist office can wait. There are some great geometrical almost abstract shots of walls, arches and empty streets requiring attention. Getting a couple of decent photos is hugely therapeutic as is the sight of a clear sky of deepest blue with a hot yellow fried egg of a sun. This imminent storm seems totally unreal. I decide to see for myself the latest weather forecast at an internet café. This confirms it would indeed be a smart move to leave Corsica asap.

I drift along to the port to check the sailings but the ticket office is closed today and tomorrow. So on to the tourist office where I'm told they do not give any information on ferries. I'll have to try one of the travel agencies. I ask about the weather. *"Tomorrow should be ok but there's a big storm on the way."* As if I didn't know....

I enter the one travel agency with its doors open this Saturday afternoon. A bright eyed young woman tells me *"hélas"* she has problems with her *"informatique"*. Her computer is down, though the last time it was up it told her tomorrow afternoon's boat to Nice was full, *"complet"*. Why don't I try down at the port?

I tell her the ticket office is closed. Which is why I'm here. *"But they open before every sailing."* Even on a Sunday? *"Oh yes, they are obliged to."* At this point I abandon my premature escape plans. The prospect of hanging around at the port on the off chance of a seat on a full ferry to Nice and then making an ignominious return to the *Grand Hotel* only to be told that room 307 is no longer *disponible* seems like the wrong option. I've taken things as far as I can, so I'll stick with my original plan. My little wobble is over.

I head back happily to the *Grand* to say I'm not leaving early after all. I'm sure Lao Tzu would approve. Anyway, what's the big deal with wind and rain? They don't do *tsunamis* in the Med. Net result of this resolution to my quandary is a sense of relief now to be in Calvi for real with a decent chunk of today and all of tomorrow at my disposal.

I resolve to make something of that. So I don baggy shorts and open sandals. A swim in the sea would be nice. But the big beach I saw from the train on the way into Calvi looked a bit crowded. A glance at the tourist map reveals a tiny bay called *Plage du Roncu*. Shouldn't take long. Back towards the Citadel then bear left and down a track to the right.

Minutes later I'm on my way. In a narrow alley I find myself behind that nice German couple from Waldshut. I am wondering how to greet them when suddenly the lady lets rip with a fart. Right old firecracker. Reverberates long and hard between the walls. You would think Admiral Lord Horatio Nelson had launched another barrage at Calvi where he famously lost an eye.

This occurred during the bloody siege of Calvi in 1794 when Nelson was fighting on the side of the Corsican patriots against the French occupying the Citadel. When a splinter from an exploding shell penetrated his eyeball, Nelson didn't make a big fuss. Writing three weeks later to inform his wife, Nelson reported that *"the slight scratch"* he had suffered *"is grown worse"* with one eye *"in almost total darkness, and very painful at times; but never mind, I can see very well with the other."* As for the siege, it ended after several weeks of intense bombardment with a French surrender. Nelson reported: *"The place is a heap of ruins."*

As for the German lady whose flatulence prompted this digression, she throws a hasty furtive glance over her shoulder to make sure no one is there, only to see me smiling sheepishly. If there had been somewhere to hide I would have done it willingly to spare her embarrassment.

Our eyes meet briefly. She is clearly mortified. I want to tell her no worries. You should have heard my grandma. She used to go like the clappers and carry on as if nothing had happened. But I don't think that will do the trick. If only for her sake I sincerely hope our paths won't cross again. Later that day I discover that Calvi has an annual *Festiventu* or *Festival of Wind*.

Plage du Roncu, when I get there, isn't up to much. The beach is a grey pebbly affair with a shallow slope, meaning a long, painful walk into water deep enough to swim. Just off to the right are some rock shelves with a few people scattered about sunning themselves. My loose fitting sandals aren't the best footwear for climbing so I tread gingerly. Accordingly I'm looking at the ground beneath my feet when I stumble across her. So it comes as a complete surprise.

A young woman, naked but for a skimpy lime green bikini bottom, lies face down on the warm rock soaking up the afternoon sun through the bronzed skin of her smooth back and lithe limbs. She may be sleeping. Her posture is far too relaxed for someone properly conscious. Her body has moulded itself languidly to every contour of the rock. She looks entirely at ease as if this were her natural habitat.

There's a delicious eroticism to the scene though it's more like a still taken from a wildlife documentary than a blue movie. It's one of those moments when the jaw goes slack. I just stand there agape for a few seconds unable to proceed. My first thought is what a great picture it would make. So beautiful and unposed: a real rock nymph caught in her private world as yet unaware of my presence.

I'm reminded of a similar moment thirty years ago while out walking the Cornwall Coast Path. I can't say offhand exactly where because during the baking hot summer of 1976 I did the whole 258 miles of it, sleeping rough in fields under the open sky. Early one afternoon in the full heat of the day on a very quiet stretch where the footpath ran through a deserted heath of parched gorse and heather bushes I found this naked couple lying spread-eagled in post-coital embrace.

Like my rock nymph in Calvi, they were enclosed in a world of their own. The man's head was resting on the woman's breast, one hand trailing on her belly. Then as now, the thought occurred to take a picture but I excused myself with a worthy pretext like respecting their privacy. Privacy? If they were using one of

England's most popular long-distance footpaths as their bedroom, what right to privacy did they have?

I can recall the scene quite accurately. Both were pale, their skin a pasty white in the blinding light like an overexposed photo. A bit longer in the sun and the soft folds of flesh would be turning pink. Not in the first flush of youth but such a tender composition, impossible to improve on its artistry. All the more endearing that they didn't have the physique of young models. This was ordinary life suspended for a precious moment of naked humanity.

I had plenty of time to take it all in since I had to figure out a way round them lying as they were right in the middle of the path. Curiously there was no sign of the clothes they had presumably cast off in the passion of the moment. But I digress…

Anyway, thirty years on, here I am again facing the same decision. To snap or not to snap? Even with three decades of professional photography under my belt I still don't have the killer instinct of the hardened photojournalist. My camera remains in its bag. As for the lady, she remains unaware of the internal debate she has inspired. She does not stir as I pass by without so much as casting a shadow across her personal space. Soon I am out of sight and safely on my way.

I put the episode out of mind as I settle down in my own secluded fold of rock as close to the water's edge as I can get. Not being a great sunbather I content myself with taking off shoes and socks, then dipping my feet in the water. I observe them as I might a pair of exotic marine creatures, bright pink in places but with a blue tinge here and there. I am even inspired to take a picture of them as they rootle about among the shingle. I soon realise paddling will not suffice. I'll have to go for the full immersion. So I strip off my clothes, bar my brightly striped boxer shorts that pass muster as swimming trunks, and crawl crablike into the sea.

Then casting caution to the wind I launch myself into deeper water where my feet won't touch any of that slimy seaweed adhering to the rocks. It's a moment of sheer bliss as I float on my back, all cares banished, happy as Larry, whoever he, or as a sandboy, whatever that. It's just me bobbing in the waves like a crouton in soup, back in the element where all human life began. I feel I have undergone a symbolic Corsican baptism.

Looking back towards the shore I note the current has carried me along to a spot just opposite the lair of the rock nymph. She is now sitting, brushing her long tresses. I'm close enough to catch glimpses of the dark buttons of her nipples standing out clearly like two dainty dishes of *crème brûlée* against the caramel tanned skin of her breasts. It's a feast for the eyes.

Aesthetics be damned, this stirs the blood more than the soul. Altogether it's a scene worthy of a naughty British seaside postcard. Elderly gent ogles bathing belle. I stay in the water much longer than I might otherwise. For form's sake I swim a few strokes out to sea then return to find the lady still there grooming herself, now attending to some small matter of pedicure. Still she shows no signs of being inconvenienced by my presence.

The sea now feels chilly. If I stay in much longer there's a risk of a cramp and then I could be swept out into choppy waters by a wayward current or slapped against the rocks. Either way unable to defend myself. What a way to go. Man lured to watery grave by the sight of naked breasts. Would make a good story in tomorrow's *Corse-Matin*. It also has the makings of a vintage *Confessions of a Tourist* piece for *The Sunday Times* except that the death of the writer poses the problem of writing the story posthumously. Perhaps that's where a ghost writer comes in?

Back to reality. Here I am treading water off *Plage du Roncu* powerless to budge from the spot as long as the lovely lady continues her *toilette*. Finally, she slips on her lime green bikini top, rolls towel under her arm and departs. Released from the spell, like a sailor that has narrowly escaped the embrace of the *Lorelei*, I scramble inelegantly back onto my own private patch of rock reflecting what a curious thing is man, ever a prey to big ideas and small lusts in roughly equal measure.

While on the subject of lust, I must confess there are advantages to getting older and no longer being constantly up for it. For a start, I'm now more tuned in to the infinitely subtle eroticisms of life than when I was a boy. Indeed I can afford to be since there is no longer an expectation or obligation to do anything about it. Not being relentlessly driven by hormonal diktat certainly clears the mind for other things.

I heartily commend Sophocles who described his senile impotence in glowing terms. Apparently, the Greek philosopher responded to the questions: *"How are you in regard to sex, Sophocles? Can you still make love to a woman?"* with the reply: *"Hush man, I am very glad to have escaped from this, like a slave who has escaped from a mad and cruel master."* Well spoken, Sophocles. Now, while I don't exactly look forward to attaining that state, I trust I will embrace it manfully when the time comes.

On the way back to the *Grand* I spot a poster announcing a concert of *Chants Polyphoniques* to be held in the cathedral this very evening. This is a real Corsican musical speciality and since I've just missed the annual festival, the famous *Rencontre de Chants Polyphoniques* in Calvi, this one small performance will do the job nicely. Plenty of time for a shower, *un petit apéritif* down by the port, then a spot of dinner. Calvi looks a much brighter prospect than on arrival.

One small sip of *Cap Corse* and my mind is off again. Actually, I'm keeping a wary eye out for any stray Foreign Legionnaires. I know that could sound bad but RG has whetted my curiosity with his mention of the nearby base of *La Légion Étrangère* and the promise of *"muscle-bound, crew-cut Rambo look-alikes swaggering around Calvi's quai Landry in their knife-edge creases and white kepis"* – and *"notoriously arrogant"* to boot.

Well here I am with a front row seat right on *quai Landry* and not one swaggering Foreign Legionnaire in sight, arrogant or not. End result is I feel curiously let down. Perhaps the lack of *Légionnaires* is because their meagre starting salary of 975 euros a month wouldn't run to that many drinks in the chic bars on trendy *quai Landry*. Or could it be that it's early to bed and early to rise in today's clean living Foreign Legion?

It's worth mentioning here that *Legionnaire's Disease* is actually named after an outbreak of the illness at a convention of the American Legion in 1976 in Philadelphia of a severe form of bacterial pneumonia. The condition, often accompanied by mental confusion, is caused by *Legionella pneumophilia* associated especially with infected water systems in buildings. So let it be put again on record that it has nothing whatsoever to with the French Foreign Legion.

Time for dinner. I head for *Piazza Crudeli*, a cosy square in front of the Baroque church of *Santa Maria*. The entire piazza has been taken over by the *al fresco* restaurant tables of two rival establishments. I toss a mental coin in the air and take a seat in the one called *Santa Maria*, named after the church.

My swim has put me in red meat mood, so to follow a starter of *salade corse* (cheese, cured pork, olives along with salady bits) I go without hesitation for the *entrecôte aux herbes du maquis*. While waiting for all that to happen I take a deep draught from a half litre china jug of AOC Corsican red, a light country wine served chilled. It slips down nice and easy. As does the starter which I seem to have eaten without even noticing it.

"*Ça a été?*"

I'm not sure of the correct response to this routine restaurant question which translates literally as

"It has been?" It's another of those unfinished, open-ended French phrases like *"Je vous souhaite…"* where you have to fill in the blanks.

In this case 'it' refers to the *salade corse* I've just devoured absent-mindedly. So how has it been? What is the missing word? Good, delicious, acceptable? Actually I think it was fairly ok which is a rather Anglo-Saxon concept and difficult to express in French. So I grunt and give a grudging nod. This seems to do the trick for the waiter takes the empty plate away, returning a few moments later with a serrated knife for the steak.

Even though I don't get a strong hit from the herbs, the meat is truly excellent and the *frites* up there with the best I've had. I round things off with a *fiadone* billed as *la vedette des gâteaux corses*. The Corsican *fiadone*, a cake made mainly of *brocciu* or cottage cheese, gets its name from a Frankish word *fladone*, which also led to the French word *flan* meaning a custard tart. I must say this Corsican cheesecake has real stellar quality.

In all, *Santa Maria* has served up a decent meal, for which I can take some credit, having brought to the table the most important ingredient: namely a healthy appetite borne of no lunch and a long swim. While waiting for the bill, I reflect that a lone diner scribbling in a notebook could be easily mistaken for a restaurant critic, one of those anonymous inspectors from *Michelin* or *GaultMillau*. Perhaps that might get me above average service, choicer portions and so on?

Then I recall a passage from *Down and Out in Paris and London* in which George Orwell documented the nasty habit of a revolutionary chef at *The Ritz* in Paris who always spat in the soup of the rich in order to make his own political point in the class struggle. Now it's not necessarily a good idea to recall such things when eating out since Orwell has made me a trifle uneasy about ordering soup in fancy restaurants, most especially any of the frothy ones like *vichyssoise*.

Down by the port I cast a glum eye over the luxury private cruisers moored along the quay. Am I envious? Must admit I wouldn't mind having enough money to afford one of these motor yachts though I hope I'd have the good taste to buy something more attractive than these floating gin palaces several of which are registered in London.

Then out of the inky blackness, emerges the bright yellow hull of a vessel in the livery of Corsican Ferries. The ship is leaving port, probably the evening sailing to Nice, as I recall from my recent researches. I've quite forgotten all about my escape plans ahead of the coming storm. Indeed, I've quite forgotten about the storm as well. I note there's hardly a breeze stirring in the calm Calvi evening and it's still shirt sleeve weather. So it all seems a lot of *angst* about nothing.

Time to make tracks for the cathedral and the concert of *Chants Polyphoniques*. While waiting for it to start I take a look at the church architecture with the help of RG who draws my attention to the grilles high up just beneath the cupola that once served to screen the lodges where Calvi's society ladies concealed themselves from the common gaze during the Mass.

Yes, there they are. I recall something similar in the older houses in Damascus and Baghdad known as *mashrabiyya* in Arabic that do much the same job of allowing ladies to peep out while preventing anyone from peeping in. Could this device be a small cultural leftover from the Moorish occupation that lasted two whole centuries during the early Middle Ages? Something cultural rather than religious that crosses the frontiers of faith. I then look around to see a lovely selection of fine-boned, attractive and intelligent female Corsican faces it would be a crying shame to conceal behind a screen of any sort.

A hush falls as the lights are dimmed. A distant echo of human voices surges forth from the chancel vault behind the altar. Steadily the singing grows in strength until the figures of four young men emerge from the shadows. Casually dressed like country folk, they might have been returning home from a walk in the hills. The music is like nothing I've heard before: an orchestra of vocal sounds that ebb and flow in a natural way without the sense of a composing or conducting hand to direct their efforts. It's magical and mysterious, the essence of spirituality as in Gregorian chanting or Russian Orthodox choirs. But the spell is broken when a saxophone, double bass, lute and guitar all join in.

Never mind, there are other distractions too. Not just the usual coughing and sneezing that are the bane of any live concert but the constant flashing of cameras as the tourists among us show the strength of their numbers. Their riotous applause after each song makes a mockery of the notice SILENCE DANS L'ÉGLISE.

My neighbour claps so loudly I have to cover both ears with my hands making it quite impossible to clap myself. But this is no bad thing since he is clapping loud enough for the two of us, just like one of the professional *claque* well-paid to applaud vociferously in an Italian opera house.

Fortunately the memory that lingers is of those amazing voices with the wings to span valleys and cross landscapes to places out of sight, out of mind. I hear the couple of encores from the back of the church and take a souvenir snap of my own, without flash if you please. I miss out on the best picture of the evening: the shadow of the fiddler dancing on the pale stone wall of the cathedral like a man possessed or some demonic character in a silhouette theatre.

I stroll down the hill to the port where a kind of rock-jazz-pop cacophony bellows forth from various bars. After the raw human energy of the *Chants Polyphoniques* it feels puny and lacking in power for all its electronically boosted volume. I know that makes me sound like an old fart. But there it is.

Sunday 24 September

I am roused from sleep shortly after midnight by the same old rock-jazz-pop cacophony still blaring up from a café just over the road. Perhaps it's to punish me for previous derogatory remarks. As consciousness returns my waking mind finds itself, for some curious reason, thinking about Benedict XVI. It takes me a few moments to figure out why.

The main item of world news on the BBC website earlier today when I checked on the progress of the storm concerned His Holiness the Pope who was still hard at work apologising for remarks made about violence and Islam in a speech in the *Aula Magna* of the University of Regensburg. It struck me at the time as an unfortunate piece of ecclesiastical diplomacy.

Now it occurs to me that this could also be a classic case of seeing the faults of others while being blind to your own. For didn't Christianity once resort to violence in the name of the one true faith? The First Crusade was launched by Pope Urban II with the battle cry of *"Deus le veult!"* or *"It is God's will!"*

Don't ask me why, but I'm unable to think of anything else while composing an alternative speech for Benedict XVI. My thought is that there's so much shared experience here in this unholy alliance of religion and violence. We've all done it, so in this sense it's something that unites rather than divides. Accordingly, it should be possible to make the general point about violence being incompatible with religion without offending anyone in particular.

Whatever the reason I have been appointed – or perhaps that should be anointed – Papal speech writer in the middle of the night, when all I want to do is sleep, I have no idea. But I have no choice in the matter. As if by divine command I take up my pen and scribble away feverishly. It takes almost an hour and I produce several pages of detailed notes. When I'm done I feel totally drained. I'm rather taken aback by my strength of feeling on this subject. I didn't think I had strong views on anything. It's not very pleasant.

This final thought is punctuated by woofing of insomniac dog and clanking bell of *Santa Maria* striking one. I am now able to rest my pen and slip into a dreamless sleep. I'm awake again at 4.30am. The music has stopped. This time it's the cheery going-home and let's-do-it-again-soon noises that have woken me.

My brain resumes its train of thought just like a computer picking up an interrupted download at the exact point it left off. But I've had enough. I decide to work no more. I resign my duties as alternative Papal speech writer. Or perhaps I have been fired? What to do with all my notes? Send them to the Vatican or consign them to my archive of unpublished writings? With that unresolved I fall asleep shortly after 5am.

At 7am a noisy detachment of German OAPs conducts an early checkout with coordinated door slamming and hearty greetings followed by a mass en-bus operation. When they are gone, calm descends once more on the *Grand Hotel*. But it's too late for sleep.

Today is going to be tricky. I check on the progress of that storm before making plans. The hotel receptionist assures me that it's still definitely on the way. But the dry weather should hold until afternoon. Well, probably, possibly. Though no guarantees either way, of course.

Then I have an idea. Can she suggest a short walk, just a few hours, half day maximum? Then poring over the map, here's me saying: *"How about to here? Is there a track?"* My finger tip rests on a promontory called *Punta Revellata*. As the meaning of the name sinks in, I think how hugely appropriate after all those thoughts during the night. *Revelation Point!* Yes, that looks just the job. How can I refuse an invitation like that?

That decided, I slip into my baggy blue shorts. Actually, they are quite a trendy number, acquired just recently from one of those designer sportswear shops. I have to admit on me they look anything but trendy with my white, sun-starved legs extending like… well like an old geezer's legs, actually.

I pop into a supermarket to pick up a bottle of water. 1.5 litres is quite a weight but the day is already hot and muggy, so better safe than sorry. While waiting at the checkout for someone to appear I flick speedily through today's edition of *Corse-Matin* just to check the weather. Looks like the hotel receptionist is right. There really is a big storm on the cards for later today.

I'm alerted by a loud cough. The manageress has been observing me from a nearby counter. Tut-tutting about some people wanting to read the paper without buying it, she refolds the copy I had opened, irons it with the palm of her hand, and replaces it further down the pile. Duly ticked off I purchase my water and a carrier bag, then exit smartly stage left.

A few doors down the road there's a *pâtissier* with some cheesy looking pastries in the window. One of those should do the trick. They are called *miacci* which sounds like a corruption of *mi piace* or 'I like that'. So I invest in a large one of those. How about some fruit? That would mean going back to face the lady in the supermarket. So I pass. Besides, I'm not after a three-course picnic lunch just enough food to nibble on as and when in order to maintain energy levels.

The prospect of this walk to *Punta Revellata* has me hooked. I'm really up for it. Not just on account of the name, though that's a definite plus. Though maybe it doesn't mean *Revelation Point* after all? No matter, it's the delicious sensation of hitting the trail, stepping out on the open road, life reduced to the simple act of putting one foot in front of the other. My legs are raring to go, straining at the leash as it were.

I think I would like to have done a travel book based on a long distance walk. Ever since I read Laurie Lee's *As I Walked Out One Midsummer Morning* the idea of striding off just for the hell of it and walking until sunset has had a strong appeal. Of course, Lee's walk had a particular point, joining the International Brigades in the Spanish Civil War. Still surely a walk almost anywhere could not fail to produce brilliant material.

Sadly, however, that is not the case. I haven't forgotten a savage review of a harmless book describing a writer's walk around the coast of Ireland. The critique began with the title of the piece *JUST WALKING* and went on from there to accuse the author of not having anything of interest to say. In fact, he was just walking. Gist of the article was he might as well have been walking the dog for all the miles he had trudged and words he had written about it. Ouch! I bet that hurt. Anyway, it put me off doing a long walk book.

Following the precise instructions of the hotel receptionist I take the main road out of town for a few hundred metres as far as a wayside cross. This is a memorial to the men, women and children, civilian and military, on board the steamer *Balkan* torpedoed off this coast during the night of 15-16 August 1918.

Already I can see across the bay to the headland of *Punta Revellata*. My pulse quickens at the sight of a lighthouse. A lighthouse! I can't see one without being instantly reminded of Virginia Woolf's best known novel *To the Lighthouse*. Although she died in 1941 a full five years before I was born, Virginia Woolf feels like an old friend. During her Bloomsbury set days she lived in Tavistock Square and Gordon Square both just around the corner from where I now live.

Apart from being regularly aware of her former presence in my neighbourhood I also once ran across her trail deep in the *Alpujarra*, a remote corner of

Andalucia where she travelled with her husband Leonard in the summer of 1923. They were there to visit Gerald Brenan, the expatriate writer and fringe *Bloomsburyite* who was then living in the village of Yegen. The thought of the literary lady at the height of her creative powers attempting small talk with the country people in their broad dialect is intriguing. I doubt they would have had more than a few words in which they could make themselves mutually understood.

Be that as it may, Virginia Woolf now pops up in Corsica. She waits calmly at my side as a fellow traveller and all because, or so I assume, there is a lighthouse at the end of my walk just as there was one at the finale of her book. There the similarities end because it needed a boat trip from Skye to a tiny Hebridean island to get to Virginia's lighthouse, whereas mine is firmly planted on the promontory of *Punta Revelleta*.

There are so many things I want to ask her, not personal stuff, like what was it like going mad and walking into the River Ouse with her pockets full of stones on what must have been a chilly spring day on 28 March 1941. Nor about being the greatest female writer of the 20th century and a trail blazer for all who followed. No, I'd just like to get her reaction to small things and see what she has to say about matters of no great consequence. Find out what makes her tick.

Should I explain to Virginia that this is a real walk and we're not going to wait a hundred or so pages before setting off? Better not. So let's be on our way. But I'm not sure she is wearing sensible shoes, and the rocks along the shore look treacherous. However, by some magic of the spirit world, Virginia seems to glide along effortlessly as if her feet aren't quite touching the ground. Fairly soon I am making heavy weather of it, even with the correct footwear, in places having to scramble rather than ramble.

Suddenly the lighthouse looks much further away. I doubt we'll get there before the storm breaks.

VW: *You see, it's not as straightforward as it looks.*

I am too stunned to reply.

VW: *Going to a lighthouse, I mean.*

These are Virginia's very own words. I seek to memorise them. She did say going to *a* lighthouse, not to *the* lighthouse, didn't she? That sort of detail could be important. I tremble with excitement. This is more than a travel writer's scoop. It's literary history in the making. Her next words form a question

VW: *Are you sure we have to take this route? There is no sign of a path. It might not lead us anywhere.*

Us? So she accepts we're in this together. That's good. Still too shy to speak, I point to the daubs of red paint on the rocks that indicate the right direction.

VW: *Looks like fresh blood. Someone has been stabbed. I expect we'll catch up soon with whoever it is. Most probably one of those nasty little Corsican vendettas.*

Cripes, what imagination! But I have to admit Virginia's idea is not so far-fetched. The *vendetta* in its original form as a remorseless blood feud between families was if not invented then certainly perfected on Corsica and Sicily. Let's hope Virginia doesn't mean it literally. Perhaps the authoress is playing with ideas, seeing life as a novel. She reads my mind.

VW: *Plots are not really my line of country. The vendetta is a good enough subject for a book, I grant you, if straightforward story telling is what you are after. But the vendetta has rather been done to death, if you'll pardon the expression, by those 19th century French writers: Honoré de Balzac, Prosper Mérimée, Guy de Maupassant, Alexandre Dumas, to name but a few.*

Oh dear, I'm not going to remember all this. I would never have imagined Virginia Woolf could be so forthcoming, downright talkative. And she does have a nice dry sense of humour. What a relief.

Our rock scrambling soon comes to an end. I'm grateful for that but disappointed the red blobs now direct us inland onto a network of roads connecting a loose sprawl of seaside villas. It's not exactly scenic or picturesque, and in places a bit smelly.

What's worse, away from the coast we've lost sight of the lighthouse. I do hope Virginia will not lose interest and drift off somewhere else. Fortunately, after a quarter of an hour or so we are back by the sea and the going gets better. Coming up ahead there's a sandy bay, with a notice announcing PLAGE PRIVÉE and a few sun beds for rent at 8 euros a day.

VW: *So this is a private beach? I don't think that should be allowed. How can the sea belong to anyone? And what precisely is a euro? Is it the local currency in Corsica?*

Too many questions all at once, so I venture to pose one of my own.

MJ: *The landscape up ahead, look over there the other side of the bay where we are going. Doesn't it remind you of somewhere? Cornwall perhaps?*

It is a genuinely spontaneous remark. Suddenly I am back on my great Cornish trek of 1976. It has the desired effect of a conversational ice breaker. Virginia is now chatting happily like a young girl.

VW: *I spent my early years in St Ives. Happy days, when mother and father were alive. We lived at Talland House. Within sight of the Godrevy Lighthouse. That's the one I used in the book. Only I transposed it to the Hebrides and placed it just off the coast of Skye. But far enough away to make the sail a risky adventure. Remarkable what a writer can do, isn't it? Moving lighthouses from one end of the country to the other. And a mere woman at that. I do hope there weren't any navigational misunderstandings on my account. The Cornish coast is treacherous at the best of times. I wouldn't want any more drownings on my conscience.*

At the mention of drowning, Virginia catches her breath. She has tripped over a bad memory. I allow the awkward moment to pass in silence. Meanwhile, I absorb and assess what she has just said.

So Virginia Woolf does stream-of-consciousness in real life, not just play with it as a literary device. It transports her to places that take her by surprise. I like that. Not always good to know exactly where you're going. Sometimes it's painful, like just now. I rapidly calculate that Virginia was 59 when she died, the same age as I am now. That's food for thought. After a few minutes silence, as if by mutual consent, I tell her briefly of my walk around Cornwall. She seems incredulous why anyone should want to do such a curious thing. My answer is pretty lame.

MJ: *Oh, just walking. Walking for its own sake…*

I don't mention the travel article I was writing at the time, nor the notebook I kept which amounted to no more than a superficial travelogue. Had it ever been published then a reviewer would have had every right to dismiss it as *JUST WALKING.*

VW: *What year did you say that was?*
MJ: *What year?*
VW: *This Cornish walk of yours?*
MJ: *1976.*
VW: *Oh, I see. A bit after my time, you understand.*
MJ: *Yes. Of course,*
VW: *You would have walked right past Talland House. It's on the outskirts of town above Porthminster beach.*
MJ: *Yes, I did. Of course, I did. I remember it well.*

This is a bare-faced lie. Truth was I passed quite a few late Victorian houses along the coast of Cornwall where I had visions of long forgotten literary folk gathering for weekend parties and writing holidays. I feel I should have made something of that Cornish walk. I could have turned it into more than just walking. I must still have the notebook somewhere. But what does it matter now?

We are both taken by surprise when a sporty young lady in the latest running gear of sexy shorts jogs past us at high speed, her *petit chien* trailing behind breathlessly at the end of a long leash. I decide on balance not to explain modern female lifestyle trends to Virginia. After all there were plenty of sporty girls in her day. Just think of that wonderful physical specimen hilariously immortalised by John Betjeman.

Pam, I adore you,
Pam, you great big mountainous sports girl,
Whizzing them over the net, full of the strength of five.

No sooner has the athletic young lady vanished from view, than an elderly gent, also well turned out in sporty running gear comes jogging along hot on her trail. Not having seen a soul for half an hour or more, it seems likely they must be together in some undefined way. But the man is old enough to be her father, so perhaps he's a sugar daddy struggling to keep advancing years at bay? Must say he seems *bien en forme* for his age.

"Don't give up, mate. She's not that far ahead. Perhaps she'll tire. You know how it is with these young fillies."

He is gone before I can utter a word. I note that Virginia is giving me a disapproving look. Maybe I've blown it just by thinking that frivolous thought? Not so, it seems, for now she is talking again.

VW: *One day walking round Tavistock Square I made up, as I sometimes make up my books, To the Lighthouse; in a great, apparently involuntary rush. One thing burst into another...*

MJ: *Tavistock Square? One of my favourite places. I live just round the corner. Isn't that a coincidence?*

I could bite my tongue with shame. Here is Virginia Woolf explaining the secret well spring of the creative process; and all I can do is interrupt her with a facile remark like that. No wonder she looks away. This time I really do think I've blown it. However, Virginia has excellent manners and takes things in her stride.

VW: *So you live in Bloomsbury? Do tell me what's going on, who's publishing what, and all about the literary scene.*

Oh dear, how to break it to Virginia that Bloomsbury is no longer the epicentre of the literary world? How to talk up the merits of chick lit and bonkbusters? What else is there to say about modern Bloomsbury? I don't suppose she wants to hear about our nice new branch of Waitrose, albeit the largest in central London. Though perhaps the recently restored railings of Gordon Square might be worth mentioning. I wonder if she recalls the beautiful bank of bluebells in the south west corner of the garden. In the end my reply is rather a let-down.

MJ: *Publishing nowadays? You don't want to know, Virginia. Believe me, you really don't want to know.*

VW: *Why on earth do you say that? Of course I want to know. I wouldn't have asked otherwise.*

MJ: *Yes, of course. I'm sorry. But that's the way we talk nowadays. What I mean is, you won't like what you hear.*

VW: *In what way?*

MJ: *Success favours the mediocre. Celebrities rule the roost. If you're famous or infamous for anything at all, publishers will sign you. Tough for genuine new authors to get noticed.*

VW: *It was rather the same in my day. Why do you think we founded the Hogarth Press? It wasn't just a hobby to keep me from going insane.*

I stumble at the unprompted reference to her fear of insanity. This was what finally drove Virginia to take her own life. She falls silent. We can now see the lighthouse in all its glory. For some reason neither of us cares to mention it. We continue on our way for several minutes without anything further being said. My next gambit comes straight off the top of my head.

MJ: *As a young man I used to attack a walk as if it were something to be despatched as quickly as possible. But now I start off with deliberate slowness, well below what my legs are capable of. I find the act of placing one foot steadily in front of the other induces a state of calm, almost of meditation. Before I know it my legs are walking of their own accord, me no longer consciously directing them. It's a sweet sensation, like riding your legs as if they were a horse or donkey.*

VW: *Your idea is of course nothing new, witness the expression 'riding Shanks's pony'.*

This takes the wind out of my sails. So I am relieved when Virginia picks up the thread.

VW: *I once rode a donkey in Spain, you know? With Leonard, in Andalucia, when we visited Brenan. Gerald Brenan.*

MJ: *Yes, I know. I read Brenan's account of that in South from Granada. I've been to Yegen too, though long after Gerald ... er, Brenan moved away.*

VW: *But all that was such a long time ago. Now what were you saying about donkeys?*

MJ: *Donkeys? Ah yes, my walking theory. I look on my legs as a donkey's legs and my feet are its hooves which find the best foothold to plant themselves, then push off with the right measure of thrust and so on. Once I'm in the groove I can go on for hours. Eventually my legs tire of course like those of any beast of burden. Then I give them a rest until they are ready to carry on. I reckon I can cover greater distances with far less fatigue than I could thirty years ago.*

Babbling on about the art of walking makes me lose concentration. I trip on some loose stones and almost come a cropper, rather ruining the effect of what I am explaining. Virginia has her eye elsewhere.

VW: *Hush! Rein in those donkey legs of yours. Look!*

We're almost there. Nearly at the lighthouse! How the miles have flown by. I can see the tip of it a short distance ahead, slightly higher than where we stand. We are looking up at it from a steep angle. Just around the next bend there's a turning to the left leading up the hill while the main path continues on the same level. No dab of red paint to guide us but we follow our noses. Five minutes later we come to a halt in front of a building with a square tower mounted on its roof bearing the name *REVELLATA* painted in large black letters on a white background.

We're here. So what now? I sense anti-climax. But Virginia is taking it all in, like an animal sniffing out a strange habitat to see if she recognises it. We make a slow tour of the building, emerging on the far side onto a large patio. An attractive dark-skinned young woman is asleep on a sun bed with headphones in her ears.

VW: *I think she must be deaf poor thing.*

No, Virginia. That's an *iPod*. She's listening to her music recorded as *MP3s*. But I decide not to challenge her innocent assumption. A young man steps out of the

French window. We exchange polite greetings. Virginia is clearly impressed by his good manners. Though the young woman arouses her disapproval.

VW: *Just look at the vacant expression on her face. You can tell the girl is in a state of non-being. What a waste of a life. Even if you can't have thoughts of your own, you can benefit from those of others. I see they have a few books on their shelves indoors. Not what I'd call a decent library. But she could at least try reading something to get the brain ticking over.*

Now we sit at a picnic table with a gorgeous sea view extending for miles over the Mediterranean to the west. Strong sensation of land's end, *finis terra*, the world stops here: an ideal spot for a shrine, chapel, oratory, hermit's cell or even a writer's retreat.

I dismiss the idea of inviting Virginia to share my lunch of lukewarm mineral water and *miacci* whose cheesy odour hits my nose as I peer into the bag. I reckon I might manage a few furtive nibbles after I've taken a picture of the view. I don't normally do views but this one is different. I take the picture with Virginia Woolf in the foreground seated at the picnic table. She doesn't appear to mind. Then she points excitedly at the spiral bound notebook tucked in the outer pocket of my camera bag.

VW: *I knew it.*
MJ: *Knew what?*
VW: *You're a scribbler.*

I nod with a suitably bashful smile.

MJ: *Not such a good one, I have to admit, with anything very much to say like...*

At the last moment I refrain from paying Virginia any superfluous compliments.

MJ: *... like anyone you may have heard of.*

VW: *No matter. A writer is a writer. Why else do you think I would keep you company?*

MJ: *The lighthouse perhaps?*

VW: *Well, yes. There is that too I suppose. I hope you don't imagine I hang around lighthouses on the off chance of sharing a walk with any old fellow countryman.*

I must confess that I find this last comment extremely gratifying.

VW: *Yes, it is entirely your responsibility, my being here. You summoned me. Simply by thinking of me. Otherwise, I could not possibly be here. You do understand?*

MJ: *Yes, of course. Thank you for coming. I am so glad you were available and ...*

I'm groping for what to say next.

MJ: *... and now we are here, what do you think of it?*

VW: *Think of what?*

MJ: *The lighthouse.*

VW: *Well, I like the name. Revellata. That's very good. Apart from that it's just a lighthouse like any other.*

MJ: *So the real point is the act of going to the lighthouse rather than arriving at the lighthouse?*

Even as I speak it, I know my question misses the point by a mile. Here I am applying the thought processes of the travel writer Robert Louis Stevenson to the intellectual authoress Virginia Woolf. I've got it totally and completely wrong.

Now how does the novel end? There's Mr Ramsay and his children at long last making the much debated trip to the lighthouse and thereby coming to terms with one another and their grief at the death of Mrs Ramsay. Then the scene shifts to the artist Lily Briscoe far away on *terra firma* putting the final touches to her big painting of land and sea and sky. Lily is achieving her artistic vision. It's a triumph, even if the resulting canvas will soon be discarded, destined to lie forgotten in some dusty attic never to be seen by the public. Yes, I think I've got it.

MJ: *So it's all about doing your creative thing? Staying true to your idea even though it brings no acclaim, no reward. Nothing. Just art for art's sake? Something like that?*

Virginia has a dreamy, faraway look. As if in a trance she utters her response.

VW: *I feel that by writing I am doing what is far more necessary than anything else.*

Far more necessary? That's a curious turn of phrase. The words are delivered with intent. But she sounds as if she is quoting someone else even though that person is in fact herself. The intensity of her expression leaves me in absolutely no doubt that for Virginia Woolf writing was as essential as breathing. Indeed more so. Here again the question of her sanity arises. I am on the point of asking her about that when she raises a finger to her lips. I am not to speak.

VW: *I have had my vision. Stay true to yours, whatever it is. Even a not so good writer must keep the faith.*

Now she is becoming transparent, almost as if evaporating in the heat of the sun. Still she speaks.

VW: *I would advise against wearing shorts. Well, not ones like those at any rate. You might look slightly less ridiculous in lederhosen or something traditional. You haven't really got the legs. Now, that Corsican gentleman we saw running along the cliff path a while back, that's an entirely different matter…*

Wth that, Virginia Woolf leaves me all alone at *Punta Revellata* staring out to sea, wondering if I haven't dreamed up the whole thing. I rub my eyes and take a deep breath.

There is a clear turning point on some trips when you reach an ultimate high, one of those truly sublime as-good-as-it-gets experiences after which inevitably things come off the boil, unwind and generally go downhill. You might not even be aware of it at the time. Only later looking back do you recognise the symbolic *nec plus ultra* point of nothing more beyond.

The first time I noticed such a thing was on an actual mountain top, the summit of Mount Misen on the small island of Miyajima near Hiroshima off the east coast of Japan. On this Corsican trip it's happening right now at 1.16pm out here by the lighthouse of *Punta Revellata*. Even without Virginia Woolf's sudden and dramatic departure I sense a distinct turning of the tide. Henceforth, it's all basically homeward bound: back to Calvi, back to Bastia, back to Blighty.

I decide to eke out the magic moment. I sit down at the picnic table to eat the *miacci* and drink some water, which I was too shy to do in Virginia's presence.

Next thing is to strip off my T-shirt now drenched with sweat, put on a cleanish shirt then drape the damp T-shirt over the bench to dry in the sun.

I desperately want to relax and think of nothing. At the same time, I feel the urge to scribble some notes while it's all fresh in my mind. In the event, I only get as far the title: *A Short Walk with Virginia Woolf.* But I leave it at that for I really don't know where to begin.

So I leave off writing and content myself with the satisfaction that I've done whatever I came here to do. Even if the rest of the Corsica trip is a complete washout, there will always be the happy experiences accumulated thus far all safely stored away in the memory bank, like a rich portfolio of digital images.

I reach for my camera to see how the shot of Virginia turned out. But it isn't there. That's not quite true. The picture exists, but Virginia isn't in it. All I have is an empty picnic table and the view from the lighthouse. Now if I were to hang this image on an art gallery wall with the title *Virginia Woolf at Punta Revellata* people would think I'm having a laugh. I'm not. She was there, believe me.

I'm not yet ready for the solitary slog back to Calvi. Doing the walk *from* the lighthouse so soon after the walk *to* the lighthouse offers no joy. I need another target to aim for. I pore over the tourist office map of Calvi which includes a few places in the surrounding area for good measure. Of these *Notre Dame de la Serra* catches my eye. The hotel receptionist had suggested it as an alternative to *Punta Revellata*. She said it was a comfortable half day there and back from Calvi. On studying the map more closely, it looks possible for me to take a cross country route direct from *Punta Revellata* to *Notre Dame de la Serra*, after which all I would have to do is make the final descent into Calvi.

The prospect of continuing on a circular walk, or a triangular one to be more accurate, is so much more exciting than a boring straight-there-and-back job. It gives me just the boost I need. Gathering up my things, I discover my sweaty T-shirt is far from dry so I carry it and let it flap in the wind. With that and my brown paper carrier bag, baggy blue shorts and white legs I must look like the sort of eccentric old buffer that sensible folk are well advised to avoid.

There are indeed other people on this path which serves as a rough vehicle track running along the spine of the headland from the main road out to the lighthouse. Thankfully, the surface is so rough that even 4x4s don't use it much beyond a certain point. The people I meet on their way to the lighthouse are fellow walkers and the occasional mountain biker.

It's a decent enough track for going from A to B with minimal risk of getting lost. But it lacks the scenic charm of the coastal path Virginia and I had taken earlier. So when I stop to reply to a rambler asking which way to the lighthouse, I am tempted to point out the merits of the picturesque route.

It really is the path less travelled, as in that poem *The Road Not Taken* by Robert Frost in which the whole point of the twenty lines of verse appears to be summed up in the closing stanza:

"Two roads diverged in a wood, and I –
I took the one less traveled by,
And that has made all the difference."

The message of the poem, however, is anything but clear. For as any walker knows, in the real world the best path is the usually the one more travelled which actually leads somewhere and hopefully to where you want to go. In any case, the real choices in life are often not paths but destinations. So it's all a bit confusing.

Apparently, the poet had no end of amusement at the various interpretations people managed to find in these deceptively simple lines. The idea of choosing the path less travelled as a guiding principle in life makes as much sense as trying to get through Hampton Court maze by always taking a left turn. All of which bears out my own feeling that the true purpose of poetry is not to simplify but to mystify.

I pause for a breather. This track seems so much longer than the one we took earlier when the miles simply dissolved beneath our feet. Now it's heavy going and my Shanks's pony is slightly knackered, knock-kneed, sagging amidships. Add to that the muggy heat, dusty road and blazing sun.

The way to *Notre Dame de la Serra* feels like one of those painful penitential acts medieval pilgrims inflicted on themselves as a scourge to their souls. But the only alternative, when I finally reach the main road, will be to walk several miles back into Calvi along the verge of a tarmac highway. So it's no contest. In this case I really must take the path less travelled. No two ways about it, if you'll kindly excuse the word play.

I can now see the main road ahead and as it gets ever closer the track is increasingly used by all manner of off-road vehicles. The last stretch is a steep climb that brings me up to a lay-by. Here a couple of mobile homes have stopped to admire the view. I join the tourists snapping the panorama of the promontory stretching out towards *Punta Revellata*.

The lighthouse is now but a tiny white fleck on the horizon. I'm impressed by the enormous distance I've covered. It's been a fair old hike and I'm glad to have that part of the walk behind me. The way ahead looks tame by comparison. A tarmac road is signposted *Notre Dame de la Serra* but only a couple of vehicles pass me as I make my way ever so slowly upwards through a weird landscape that gets weirder with every bend.

Finally, I simply have to stop and take a picture of the unreal rock formations that might have been designed for or by Salvador Dalí. Like human skulls or massive dinosaur eggs with bits missing, they are arranged in a grand composition as if for one of those art-in-the-landscape projects. Then I catch sight of the dome of *La Chapelle de Notre Dame de la Serra* – welcome reassurance that I'm almost there.

At this point I experience one of those sublime moments that can redeem the worst of journeys, although today it comes as the icing on the cake. Just off to the left there's a simple stone structure built against the side of the hill. Water trickles gently out of a spout and drains away through a small pool. As if this isn't clear enough, there's a helpful explanatory notice in Corsican: *FUNTANA D'ACQUA*. Excellent!

For one of the things my Cornish walk taught me was to use every opportunity to bathe my feet in the clear, cool water of a wayside stream. It offers a sensation not far short of rebirth or at any rate a healing balm that allows the limping long-distance walker to put a few more miles on the clock.

There's a handy stone ledge on which I spread out my affairs in comfort. Off come boots and socks, in go feet under the refreshing spring. I lean back against the stone wall to savour the delicious tingle spreading through my body. I peel off my shirt damp with sweat, wash head, shoulders, armpits and whatever else I can reach of my torso. Then I lean back to dry off in the sun. It's just wonderful when the need of the moment is so basic and elemental it can be satisfied by a mere trickle of cool water. Sheer bliss.

I notice I'm not alone. A tribe of small green and black lizards that must have rushed for cover when I burst in on their patch have now decided it's safe to venture forth and go about their business. A couple investigate my socks simmering in the sunshine but they're not impressed. The longer I stay still the bolder the lizards become. Close up on the wall next to my head at eye level I can see the internal quivering spasms that cause them to tremble; and the little stamping movements they make with their front feet. Is this a warning or a greeting?

I feel I could almost start talking to them. That would be a fresh take on the legendary deeds of St Francis communing with the birds in Assisi. If I linger any longer I fear I'll be going soft in the head.

So after a half hour I pack up my gear, put on socks and boots, then leave *FUNTANA D'ACQUA* to its rightful owners. With a fresh pair of feet it's now like walking on air as I cover the final few hundred metres to *La Chapelle de Notre Dame de la Serra*.

The chapel itself, an 1860s structure replacing the 15th century sanctuary, is locked. Having come all this way I feel slightly cheated until I take in the absolutely stupendous view from the belvedere down towards Calvi. There's a long low wall just perfect for taking the weight of one's feet so I duly sit down and drink in the panorama. So far it's been a sensational day and still no sign of that storm as I gaze out to the north west, from which quarter it is due to approach.

I count my blessings that I didn't do a runner on the afternoon ferry to Nice which I can see even now moored in the protective embrace of the port beneath the Citadel. Strange to think I had my escape route all planned out in my head. On arrival in Nice I would go straight to the station and book myself an overnight *couchette* to Paris. Next morning I'd breakfast somewhere on the *Rive Gauche* with views of the Seine. After that head to *Gare St Lazare* and take a train to Dieppe. Why Dieppe? Because that was my very first taste of 'abroad' where our school trip landed on French soil off the Newhaven ferry way back in the 1950s.

So strong were my expectations of France I really expected the ground beneath my feet actually to feel somehow different, perhaps charged with some exotic energy. But there was nothing. It was just the same as back home in England. First disappointment.

Ah, but it's only a concrete dock, I told myself and waited for a chance to dig my toes into the genuine native earth. That evening we headed south by night train, our destination Arles. As dawn broke I peeped through the blinds at the Provence countryside looking just like a Van Gogh landscape with cypress trees and wind breaks of bulrushes from the Camargue. Ah yes, that was the real deal. A moment to savour.

Accordingly, it occurred to me a sentimental journey to Dieppe would be a bonus to my Corsican jaunt. Interesting to see the town properly. My only memories from the school trip were of endless walks along huge docks lugging overweight suitcases into massive sheds where *douaniers* treated us to such a thorough inspection we might have been alien invaders; and those big suitcases we had to lug about were enough to put you off travel for life.

Now here's a question. If the wheel was invented thousands of years ago, why was it only recently that people realised it made sense to attach a pair of them to luggage? I think we had landed men on the moon before we got around to putting wheels on suitcases. Do we have the porters' union protecting jobs to thank for that delay? Anyway, how we suffered as kids. And how illogical is the course of human progress.

Such thoughts flit through my head as the Nice ferry detaches itself from the jetty down in Calvi and slowly heads out to sea. That's my escape route going, going, gone. Again I breathe a sigh of relief I am not on that boat. Or else I would not have done this walk. I had thought this Sunday might be a real drag, kicking my heels, trying to pass the time between lunch and dinner dodging the rain by hopping from bar to bar.

So I watch with complete equanimity as my ship departs. I really don't mind if I do get stranded here. Corsica feels good. Somehow I'm right in my element, whatever that mysterious dimension is. I also appear to have overcome my island phobia, the fear of getting stuck indefinitely. Remains to be seen, however, if that will hold good elsewhere on another island.

This *rêverie* is interrupted by a youth over-revving a very noisy motorbike. I am tempted to shout: *"Foutez-moi la paix!"* But I can't be bothered. Then a French couple want their picture taken. It has to be just so, they explain, with them here and the view of Calvi there. *Voilà!* That done to their entire satisfaction, they having checked the result before letting me go, I am immediately engaged for the same shot by a pair of German cyclists, who seem to think I know what I'm doing. Actually I do. So I click away once more. Two grinning young men in lycra shorts proudly clutching high tech bikes with so many gears they can probably ride up the side of a house. Click, click.

"Danke schön."
"Bitte schön."

So to practical matters. I try to see which of the various footpaths will take me back to base. It's really impossible to tell. It's not a simple choice between two, as in the Robert Frost poem. Real life as ever is more complex than art. Without a map it's pure guesswork. Important to get this right, a wrong turn would mean having to retrace my steps back up a very steep hill.

The German cyclists are ready to set off. I know from our chat they too are heading for Calvi. They've mounted a miniature videocam to one of the bikes to film the descent. I watch them set off. I reckon all I have to do is see which route they take then follow on at my own pace. Should be easy enough to spot them in those bright blue vests.

Yes, there they are. But they quickly disappear behind a large rock after which I catch one more brief glimpse of two bolts of blue like a pair of kingfishers before they are swallowed up in the woodland. Actually I think kingfishers are generally to be seen singly, but I'll let this simile stand.

Well, I reckon I have the general direction in my head and so I make ready to leave *Notre Dame de la Serra*. No problem getting as far as the large rock after which it's a case of flipping a coin. What I'm now after is the path more travelled but there is no obvious candidate. Then something catches my eye. Isn't that the flaked and faded remains of a spot of red paint on that boulder down there? Yes, I've found the right track. I take it with some confidence.

Ten minutes further down I meet two red-faced German cyclists carrying their bikes uphill. *"Too steep and too many rocks for bikes. OK for walkers."* They explain their painful retreat with embarrassment. We part company and I press on down what is indeed a steep, narrow and rocky path, in places almost a scramble. At last it evens out and I emerge from the trees to catch another distant view of Calvi now from a much lower angle.

Back at the *Grand Hotel* I'm eager to tell the hotel receptionist all about my exploits. She will surely be impressed with my 6-hour triangular tour. If so she is not letting on. Never mind. A shower and a shave are enough to restore me. Half an hour later, I'm down at a café on *quai Landry* sipping a frosted glass of *Cap Corse* and reading the newspaper.

There's an astounding article in today's *Corse-Matin* that immediately grabs my attention. A lady gynaecologist Danièle Flaumenbaum has just published a book *FEMME DÉSIRÉE, FEMME DÉSIRANTE* which translates literally as *WOMAN DESIRED, WOMAN DESIRING*. The work calls into question one of the great popular myths about France, namely that the French know all there is to know on the subject of *l'amour* which in this context means sex.

According to Flaumenbaum, whose observations are based on no less than 30 years clinical experience, most of her female patients have never experienced orgasm and 85% don't get full pleasure or indeed no real pleasure, from sex. This tallies broadly with the well known line of singer Georges Brassens *"95 fois sur cent, la femme s'emmerde en baisant"*, or 95 times out of a hundred a woman gets bored making love.

Flaumenbaum blames this partly on Catholic morality which defines women in one of three simple categories as mother, virgin or whore. She argues that there's also a bourgeois prudishness permeating French society that has an effect on sexual attitudes. So where does that leave the proverbial French sexiness, all that *flirtitude*, those outrageous *liaisons dangereuses*, the daring *ménage à trois* and good old *soixante-neuf*? It's a sobering realisation that French women are *sexuellement fermées*.

Flaumenbaum admits to being a victim of the same *malaise* as a young woman: *"I didn't know how to live life fully as a sexualised woman until my forties."* She's not pulling her punches when she states her belief that young girls should no longer be taught that the vagina is just there for reproduction and childbirth. Rather its prime purpose is to receive the male penis and derive sexual pleasure. Yes, pregnancy and procreation may follow from that. But the pleasure of sex comes first.

Interestingly, Flaumenbaum maintains that it's not a question of men having to improve their sexual technique, locate the magic G-spot and so on. Rather it's down to women to tap into the well spring of their own sexuality and then let themselves go for whatever takes their fancy. The book is a runaway best-seller and if its message is embraced then France could well be a very exciting country to visit in years to come.

Meanwhile, still no sign of even one Foreign Legionnaire down here on *quai Landry* so I'll have to give up on that. For dinner I head back to *Piazza Crudeli* in front of the church of *Santa Maria*. This time I cross the square to check out the competition at *Chez Doumé*. With *la fin de saison* just a week away at the end of September the staff are distinctly demob happy, so service is a bit sloppy but still OK.

I get friendly enquiries of *"Ça allait?"* as I finish the starter of grilled vegetables and *"Ça se passe bien?"* as I struggle through an enormous portion of *sauté de veau aux olives*. It finally dawns that the one correct response to all such questions is a simple *"Merci."*

Afterwards, down to the port to walk off the dinner and sip a *digestif*. There's a notice at the ferry office informing that the evening sailing to Nice has been cancelled on account of the bad weather. Next possibility will be tomorrow afternoon from Bastia.

A man behind me has just read the notice and explodes with anger and frustration. It's a crash course in French swearing, a hugely impressive performance. All to no avail. When he has given vent to his feelings he can do nor more than wave his arms theatrically and trudge off dragging an enormous suitcase.

I feel like telling him at least his suitcase has wheels. He should be thankful for that. But he looks too dangerous to approach. The elegant lady at his side now drops a couple of paces behind him. Presumably they have checked out of their hotel and must attempt to check in again. For there is no way out of Calvi this evening by any form of public transport.

So this storm is finally for real. That means my last couple of days on Corsica will be a complete wash out. Perhaps the train won't run if there's a landslide somewhere on the line. Then I too will be stuck in Calvi. Perhaps I should have taken that afternoon boat. I could be in Nice right now with a *couchette* booked for the night. Wake up tomorrow in Paris.

But then I wouldn't have had that amazing walk to the lighthouse with Virginia Woolf. I have to admit it was worth coming here just for that. Still, now that's done I really wouldn't mind drawing a line under my Corsica trip, especially since our sea links to *le continent* have been sundered. My island phobia is back.

With these dark thoughts I regain the solitude of room 307 and sort out my packing ahead of an early start tomorrow. As I switch off the light and settle down I become aware of a load of drunks braying like demented donkeys from a café down below as they belt out their tuneless songs. Sounds like the lads are celebrating a football victory or suchlike. Even with windows and shutters closed it's quite a racket. Looks like I am in for another long, sleepless night.

Monday 25 September

The great storm arrives at last. Wind and rain lash the *Grand Hotel*, rattling shutters and drumming on the window panes, arousing me from my slumbers at 3.17am precisely. So the tempest is here at last and doing its stuff. Let it blow itself out and get the worst out of its system while I'm safely tucked up in bed for the next few hours.

Meanwhile, thoughts turn to practical matters. How can I get to the station without a total drenching? For I have no umbrella and no waterproof of any description. When I packed my bag back in London the internet forecast showed only bright sunshine for the five days from Wednesday to Sunday. I took a gamble that Monday would be no different, but the change couldn't be more dramatic.

Corsica begins to feel like a devious trap that has bided its time. Now it's finally been sprung. If I had only listened to that inner voice and taken the ferry I would now be in a high speed train more than halfway to Paris. I think back to *Punta Revellata*. What must it be like out there at the tip of the headland right now, blowing a gale? I shudder to think.

One good thing about the storm. If the drunks in the café are still singing, I can't hear them. Not that I can sleep anyway with the tempest howling. At 4.46am

I get up and look for something to do. Too tired to read, I end up studying my boots lying on the floor.

They remind me of that Van Gogh painting *Boots with Laces*. So I take some pics. Then I fall asleep for almost an hour sitting in the armchair. Wake up with a stiff neck. It's like being back at Gatwick Airport all over again. Meanwhile, there's a comfortable bed over there that's costing me 84 euros a night.

I sense things are unravelling fast. No matter what I do, there'll be no stopping whatever it is from happening. It's like being in a bad dream. I'm running through treacle and the harder I try to go fast the slower I get. I drag myself back to bed and doze fitfully until the alarm goes off at 6.15am.

Night porter looks like he hasn't slept a wink. He's none too interested in hearing let alone respond to my platitudes about the storm. In his job he must have had as many meaningless conversations about the weather, both good and bad, as any man alive. Not that he looks that alive. Ashen faced, clearing his chest with a deep rumble of phlegm in the bronchial tubes. Bet he's suffering from those early morning smoker's pains I once knew all too well. He'll feel better after he's got his first cigarette butt in the ashtray. Sure enough, out comes the packet. Now he smiles. Yes, I can go up for breakfast in about ten minutes.

After checkout the rain holds off long enough for me to make it to the station. Things are looking up. Maybe today won't be such a disaster. Only half a dozen or so other passengers wait on the platform. A short distance away in a siding there's our train being checked over by the driver/engineer. That's the good thing about a railway terminus. Trains are generally there ahead of departure so you can relax, board at leisure with no unseemly rush.

Here she comes now, snuggles up gently against the buffers. I make quite sure which is the direction of travel then grab a decent seat in the first row on the left for the sea view. The driver sits amidships on what looks like a large bar stool mounted on a pedestal. I have a clear view to his left through a window freshly washed by the storm. Clear that is, until the conductor installs himself right there. Even so I have a pretty good sight of the track ahead over his shoulder.

Dawn is just breaking on a blustery, grey day as we pull out of Calvi at 7.23am, right on schedule. I look back across the bay to the Citadel. Even on this dull overcast morning it's a fine sight. Beyond that to the west, from far out on the headland, *Punta Revelleta* flashes her blinking light like a fond farewell. No point saying goodbye to Virginia Woolf. She'll be safely home in Bloomsbury by now or chatting to some other aspiring writer with a lighthouse on his mind.

We amble out along the coast at the speed of a tram on the Blackpool seafront. The weather is pretty much what you'd expect to find in Lancashire at this time of year. Brightening sky soon darkens, as if the sun has changed its mind. Diesel oil smells perfume the air. Not unpleasant. Driver and conductor a companionable pair chatting non-stop all the way.

At Algojola the conductor almost loses his head by sticking it out of the door at precisely the same instant the driver presses the button to close it. Ouch! He needs both hands to hold back the door while he wiggles his head back to safety. He's making a joke of it now but from the way he's rubbing his neck it was a near thing. Both men are casually dressed in blue jeans and T-shirts. No fancy railway uniforms here. Corsica isn't Switzerland.

We turn inland after Île Rousse. The scenery gets indeed to feel a bit Swiss. There are cows on the line at Novella. Amusing to see their startled faces as they make their escape. One bovine doesn't know which way to turn. So it stands there confused, planted like a tree in the middle of the track. Only when the train has stopped does she make a rather undignified exit.

In Ponte-Leccia the driver and conductor change ends. I'm now riding backwards to Bastia with the track unfurling behind the train like two parallel strands of steel from an enormous bobbin. So I have my face to the past, my back to the future, savouring the good old Maori View again.

Much confusion at Casamozza. A railway official seems intent on preventing us from completing our scheduled journey to Bastia. After lengthy discussions on the platform, our train is ordered straight back to Calvi. Passengers are requested to disembark and wait for another connection. Fortunately, it's not long in coming and soon we are on our way again.

As a committed urbanite my pulse quickens at the approach of Corsica's largest city. On arrival at the station in Bastia, a young local woman asks me of all people where we are. *"This is Corte, isn't it?"* In the confusion at Ponte-Leccia she took the train instead of the rail replacement bus. Still she doesn't seem too put out by the four hour wait for the next train back.

Bastia part two feels strangely familiar. I even recognise the mosaic design on the station floor and the *graffiti* outside like old friends. It has been raining very heavily to judge from all the puddles. But now there's nothing more than a light drizzle in the air.

So I head on foot for *Hôtel Central* where I have a booking. It turns out not quite as central as *Hôtel des Voyageurs* which has one of those classic names that should be slapped on a film or a novel. Though the one that really takes my fancy, as I wheel my suitcase down *Avenue M. Sébastiani*, is *Hôtel Univers*.

With a grandiose name like that it's a two star of course. Your average *Hôtel Univers* always has ideas way above its station. That's an essential part of the charm. Just seeing the name conjures up memories of countless other versions of *Hôtel Univers* scattered all over France.

I think what a lovely photographic project that would have made. I say 'would have' because these modest establishments, until quite recently invariably shabby, down-at-heel, oozing period charm and gritty character, have now all been renovated, updated, modernised, sanitised and generally homogenised into a bland universal formula. This *Hôtel Univers* in Bastia is no exception. Nostalgia aside, I must confess I prefer the new vision when it comes to wanting somewhere clean and pleasant to spend the night.

Hôtel Central turns out to be a good choice. Young man on reception quickly finds my booking, takes the outstanding payment on a credit card, gives me the key a full hour ahead of the official time, recommends a few local restaurants, lends me an alarm clock and even programmes a wake up call on the phone in my room as a back up.

The early start is because I've opted for the 6.10am bus to Bastia Airport tomorrow morning. It's only a ten minute walk to the stop outside the *Préfecture*. If recent experience is anything to go by then I'll be wide awake anyway so I might as well get moving. So that leaves me the rest of today for Bastia.

First stop is the *Oratoire de l'Immaculée Conception* and a quick history lesson. The church was used during the short-lived Anglo-Corsican kingdom from 1794 to 1796 for parliamentary sessions under the English Viceroy Sir Gilbert Elliot. This unlikely political marriage of interests was embraced by the Corsican patriot leader Pascal Paoli to safeguard Corsica against both French and Italian ambitions.

In the event, Paoli rapidly became unhappy with British control over Corsican affairs. When he made his position clear, Sir Gilbert saw fit to have him exiled. As a result the Paoli loyalists went straight over to the French side, forced Sir Gilbert and his British troops to pull out, leaving Corsica wide open for France to snap it up. So you could say that today's French Corsica is all down to the British making a right old bungle.

I wander through some quietly elegant streets near *Place du Marché*, in its present autumnal mood rather Parisian. I'm taking it nice and easy as if walking an imaginary dog. Meanwhile, others have recently been exercising their very real *petit chiens* to judge by the collection of turds on the *trottoir*.

The overall standard of presentation is right up there on a par with Paris. One has an amazing orange hue as if the little bow-wow had been on a diet of raw carrots. I'm even tempted to take a photo. The urge soon passes. Then there's a rather sophisticated work where one turd has been coiled artfully on top of another. That must have been tricky. Perhaps they are holding a competition. There might be a fortune to be made breeding a dog with artistic toilet manners.

The rain thickens to a steady drizzle as I climb a staircase leading up through *Jardin Romieu* towards the old walled city. The thin coating of water on the steps brings out some subtle colours in the stone. I stop to take a picture. The narrow streets of *Terra Nova*, as this part of Bastia within the ancient citadel is called, are largely traffic free and residential. It's all eerily quiet.

The big attraction in this part of Bastia, the *Musée d'Ethnographie Corse*, is currently closed for renovation. So instead of that I explore the churches of *Terra Nova*. First up is the *Oratoire Ste-Croix*, 16th century chapel with a rich interior decorated *à la Louis XV*. It's like a fancy jewel casket with every surface adorned in heavenly blue and bright gold: a celestial vision. It's so different when you gaze into the vault of a Gothic church where it's all about form and structure with pointed arches directing the eye and the mind upwards to God.

I think I'm on to something here. While Gothic functions like a signpost to heaven, Baroque serves you up paradise on a plate with its domes covered with billowing clouds against a sky of ethereal blue all aflutter with angelic *putti* defying the laws of gravity. But a church can be only a metaphor of heaven not the real thing. I'm less inspired by the *Cathédrale Ste-Marie* but it keeps me out of the weather for a bit.

When the rain eases I venture forth. South of the cathedral there's a plaque on a house informing that Victor Hugo lived here as a child from 1803 to 1805. I first got to know Hugo as a verbose 19th century French poet and rediscovered him many years later as the author of the blockbuster novel *Les Misérables* which became the world's longest running musical.

Given the length of the novel which runs to well over a thousand pages in the Penguin edition translated by Norman Denny, a lot had to be omitted in the stage version. An obvious candidate for the chop was the 45 page long digression on the Battle of Waterloo which has gone down in French literary history as the first time the word *merde* appeared in print.

The tragic scene at Waterloo according to Victor Hugo's account in *Les Misérables* is of utter desperation for a small group of beleaguered French soldiers. With the battle already lost they have formed themselves into a tight defensive square. Their aim is to go down fighting. They regroup time and again as their numbers diminish under a furious assault from the British. The situation is clearly hopeless. Further resistance would be sheer suicide. Honour has been amply satisfied. What is the point of more deaths? Finally, one of the British generals calls out: *"Brave Frenchmen, will you not surrender?"*

At this point one man steps up to the plate. Thus Pierre Jacques Étienne Cambronne, the French officer in command, passes out of obscurity and into the realm of immortality by responding to the call for surrender with his defiant cry of *"Merde!"*

So the British open fire and the last of the French defenders are mown down. Cambronne is badly wounded but does not die. At this point Victor Hugo takes poetic flight, waxing lyrical on the epic value of this one word which he describes as *"perhaps the greatest ever uttered by a Frenchman."* He continues: *"The real victor of Waterloo was not the defeated Napoleon, or Wellington, who was so nearly defeated, or Blücher, who scarcely fought; it was Cambronne."* There is something supremely French about the idea that a single word, and one meaning excrement or just plain shit, can wrest something heroic and uplifting from an abject defeat. Bravo!

In real life Cambronne survived to tell his own contrasting version of events. He denied, perhaps out of modesty, having used the M word at Waterloo. But the legend was more powerful than the truth. It rapidly became such a firm part of national folklore that Cambronne's name even served as a euphemism for *merde* in expressions such as *"What a load of old Cambronne!"* You'll still find *le mot de Cambronne* listed in a French dictionary as meaning a load of shit.

In one final twist, such as only real life can supply, Cambronne ended up marrying Mary Osburn, the Scottish nurse who cared for him after Waterloo. That little episode on its own suggests distinct dramatic possibilities: *MERDE! – THE MUSICAL!* Now wouldn't that be something?

I scribble this in the *Cathédrale Ste-Marie* while outside the rain continues to fall. Dodging the downpour in Bastia has become a real game of cat-and-mouse. So far I haven't done too badly but I'm increasingly aware of a chill dampness spreading downwards from my shoulders. I'm now a long way from the hotel and time is moving on. I'll have to make a dash for it sooner or later. A few minutes later the rain dries up to a feeble drizzle so I seize my chance. I'm pretty sure the worst is over as I step out onto the gleaming wet cobbles and inspect the sky.

Yes, why not? I opt for the scenic route back, taking in a spur of the jetty by the *Vieux Port* in order to see what the view is like from that angle. I am striking out confidently to the extremity of the *Jetée du Dragon* when I stop in my tracks at the sight of a simply enormous pair of lady's knickers pegged to a washing line on the deck of a yacht. I've never seen anything so large. They might serve as an additional sail.

I am fumbling for my camera when suddenly the wind gets up and the bloomers flap about wildly as if straining at the leash. Then just as I am about to take my snap, a powerful gusts pops the pegs and off they fly over the port of Bastia. I can only look on in amazement as they flutter off at high speed in the blustery wind to a destination unknown.

At this point the sky darkens and down comes the rain. I'm a sitting duck out here in the open. In fact, better pretend I am a duck for all the good an umbrella or raincoat would do me now. Within two seconds I'm drenched to the skin. Fortunately, the air is pretty warm so it's bearable. I struggle back to the relative shelter of the trees overhanging the high walls of the *Jardin Romieu* where I stand hunched with a folded newspaper over my head. A minute of this is enough to convince me I might as well continue on my way.

Back at *Hôtel Central* I drape wet clothes over the furniture wherever I can. I could do with a drink but I can't risk another drenching or I'll have no dry clothes left at all. I'm really travelling light on this trip. Nothing for it but stay here and wait for the rain to clear up. So I bide my time and catch up with today's news in a very soggy copy of *Corse-Matin*. The newsprint almost disintegrates between my fingers.

The lead story splayed across the front page concerns 100 kg of explosives destroying a villa in Porticcio. I turn to page 5 for details. At around 13.15 yesterday a massive explosion shook the south shore of the Gulf of Ajaccio. The noise was heard downtown followed by a 30 metre high column of smoke visible from a long way off. The target was the luxury holiday home of Belgian press baron Marcel Leempoel, owner of the magazine *Ciné Télé Revue*.

The bombs went off during the owner's absence. So fortunately, no fatalities or injuries. With a hastily daubed inscription the FLNC claims the credit. The acronym, working obligingly well both in Corsican and French, stands for *FRONTE DI LIBERAZIONE NAZIUNALE DI A CORSICA* or *FRONT DE LIBÉRATION NATIONALE DE LA CORSE*

Corse-Matin reports that the explosives placed in the basement of the house were strong enough to lift the roof and send debris flying over the coastal road much used at weekends by Ajaccio locals heading out for a Sunday picnic. Given the timing of the explosion it was indeed fortunate that no one was hurt.

When Edward Lear visited Ajaccio in the 1860s he asserted the view that on a wet day it would be hard to find a duller place. Well, you can hardly say the same today. I wonder if Miss Campbell were alive today and running her *Cyrnos Palace Hotel*, would her establishment receive the attentions of the FLNC? I can't imagine her taking things lying down.

I turn to page 3 of *Corse-Matin* where a smiling, bronzed and moustachioed Daniel Auteuil is pictured doing the honours at the closing ceremony of a small film festival held recently in Porto-Vecchio. One of France's highest profile celebrities the actor has a house in Corsica where he spends four to five months a year.

In the brief Q&A interview Auteuil stresses that this house is his *résidence principale* and that he would spend even more time in Corsica if he could. I wonder if this is his discreet way of reminding the gentlemen of the FLNC that he is a proper Corsican resident, not to be confused with one of those second home owners?

Perhaps Auteuil's place of birth gives him a special identity, for he is not geographically speaking even from *le continent*, having been born on 24 January 1950 in Algeria. So he's a French national but not actually from France, rather like some Corsicans see themselves. Oh, and one more thing, Auteuil has just played Napoleon in an Italian film entitled *Napoléon et Moi* that casts France's great emperor as a dodgy wheeler-dealer in the mould of Sylvio Berlusconi.

Still raining outside. At least I'm better off than Charles Trenet singing his cheery song while it was actually raining in his room:

"Il pleut dans ma chambre
J'écoute la pluie
Douce pluie de septembre
Qui tombe dans mon lit."

I can't stay here for ever. Wonder if the hotel can lend me an umbrella? Chap on reception was very helpful. But now behind the desk there's a lady of a certain age with a nothing-gets-past-the-concierge look all over her face. Immediately I know I'm on to a loser. Yet I play my hand, poor as it is.

"Bonsoir, Madame. Vous n'auriez pas un petit parapluie…?"

No need to finish the question. That's one thing I've learned on this trip.

"Un petit parapluie…?"

She repeats my words ironically, complete with the three dots preceding my tentative question mark. Then she chuckles to herself as if to say it's the best joke she's ever heard. She adds nothing more but her expression says it all. She? Lend me? An umbrella? I must admit it's pretty funny too and I convey this with a Gallic shrug that means: *"I thought you'd like that one…"*

Back in my room I consult RG on where I might eat in Bastia this evening and I come across a few lines on *Hôtel Central*. It gets a very good write up as does the welcoming *patronne* Madame de la Paillonne who *"runs a tight ship"*. Makes me wonder if RG also asked for the loan of *"un petit parapluie…?"*

Come 6pm I'm bored and restless in rainy Bastia as was Edward Lear in Ajaccio 140 years ago. Checking the weather from the window for the umpteenth time, I convince myself it's easing off. In any case it's time for a drink and a bite to eat.

I've decided to go for *Le Bouchon* right on the *Vieux Port*. Gets a good mention from RG. Chap on reception recommended it too. Can't take pot luck with my own restaurant research on a night like this. Final glance at *Corse-Matin* confirms bad weather cancelled yesterday's Nice-Calvi-Nice crossing, orange alert in Bastia until noon today, things calming down after that.

I head down to *Place St-Nicolas*. Not only has the sky cleared, but there's a big rainbow spanning the port. I postpone my *apéritif* to take some snaps. There's a great one of the Napoleon marble statue framed in the bright arc of the spectrum as if being drawn up into heaven. The large bulk of the ferry *Napoleon Bonaparte* is momentarily bathed in evening sun. Better snap that too. She'll be sailing soon at 20.00 on the slow overnight crossing to Marseille. Looking up at her flags and pennants gaily fluttering in the breeze, I wonder if those fly-away bloomers I saw earlier might be keeping them company. If so they'll be over the water on the French mainland by morning.

 Once again, I get an almost physical tug at the heart. I want to be sailing away. I ache to be on that ship, not going back to *Hôtel Central*. But that's a dream, so I repair to *Café de la Paix* for a glass of *Casanis* the local *pastis* popularly known as a *casa* when ordering one in a bar. I do precisely that and the waiter fetches me a shot of the brown liqueur turning milky as the ice cube melts. I feel I am starting to do justice to Bastia. So I have another *casa* to help things along until dinner. Finally, I reckon it's OK to head for *Le Bouchon*.

 Now I must hurry on account of some big, fat raindrops falling on my head. I reach the as yet empty restaurant at precisely 7.53pm. I'm quite sure of the time because I check my watch when the waitress standing before me says they don't open until 8pm. Her body language defies me to take one more step in her direction let alone dare to sit down and ask for a drink to while away the 7 minutes still on the clock.

 Vowing not to return, I back off into the wet night. The rain is getting serious. Next door a pizzeria is doing a roaring trade. Waiter shows me to a table. Only now do I realise I'm not actually indoors but under an awning leaking in several places from the powerful onslaught of the storm. Then I look down to see the pavement beneath the tables awash with rainwater streaming towards the gutter outside. I decide on balance *Le Bouchon* is the better option. To this day I am not sure if that was the correct choice.

Shortly after 8pm I push open the door of *Le Bouchon* with some misgivings. I feel like a spectator in my own bad dream trying to warn myself: *"Stop! Don't do it!"* Meanwhile, the other me, the material person, stands already in the dragon's den. The waitress is quite civil as she directs me to a table. It doesn't look too comfortable squashed up against the high counter beyond which is located the chef's open-plan kitchen. One wayward blow on the chopping block and a chunk of something bloody could easily land on my head. It's also right where the waitress will be squeezing past with all those dishes both full and dirty.

The restaurant is still empty, so I resolve the matter simply by installing myself at another table. To her credit, the waitress takes this in her stride. Though when I ask her to decipher an item on the handwritten blackboard I get this look that tells me I'm a lazy pupil who shouldn't need help with his reading. Ironically, the chef's favourite tunes now playing in the kitchen include the original rendering of that ghastly song: *"Hey, teacher, leave those kids alone…"*

In the end I order a simple pork chop with two veg. Having declined the various starters I am then invited or rather informed that I must order a dessert in advance. I always hate having to guess before starting a meal how I would like to finish it, so I decline the dessert as well.

Didn't RG say this was an *"easy-going"* wine bar? Even getting a glass of wine proves a hassle, there being no house red available in a *carafe* or *pichet* but minute measures of various pricier items which are poured somewhere behind the scenes where you can't see the label let alone the bottle.

I'm amazed how fast *Le Bouchon* fills up. So they really don't need my custom at all. Soon even the awkward table I had rejected is occupied by a young couple. I note that they have to keep elbows well tucked in and heads down. Other folk, I can report, are also put through the mill should they request help reading the blackboard. A lady enquires about the same item I had struggled with. It turns out to be *pague*. Never heard of it. Doesn't sound that appetising. Then she asks about the *turbot rôti au couscous*.

In truth it's not really a question so much as an invitation for the waitress to describe the dish and talk her into ordering it. Instead, the waitress asks the customer exactly what it is she wants to know, the subtext being which word is it you don't understand: *turbot, rôti* or *couscous*? At this point I wonder why people think it's such fun to eat out in cramped, crowded restaurants and be casually insulted for their pains. I conclude that it's not only the English who have the masochistic taste for ritual humiliation.

All this carping is unfair. The waitress is on her own, clearly rushed off her feet, just running hard to stand still. The chef is a one man band too. As for the food, the pork chop turns out to be a wise choice, tasty and succulent, served with a neat little salad of exotic green leaves topped with roasted almonds and a tangy dressing. But the *sauté* potatoes disappoint, too soft and oily for my liking.

I pay my bill and step out into the blustery night. I might sound disgruntled but actually I'm not. I'm still enjoying Bastia. I even take positives out of *Le Bouchon*. For example, the tiny measures of wine will save me nursing a hangover. So I'm feeling better already. At last the rain has stopped so I take the longer walk back along the waterfront. Almost immediately, I come across a place that has friendly service and good value written all over it. Ah well, that's life.

Back at *Hôtel Central* I find myself in pensive mood. My trip is basically over and I'm still no nearer to getting answers to my questions. What is the point of travel? What is the point of writing about it? I notice a stack of *National Geographic* magazines piled up on the bedside shelf. Maybe some clues in there?

At random I come across the hair-raising account of a group of American scientific explorers who made a year-long trek on foot through the swamps and forests of darkest equatorial Africa, running the gauntlet of poisonous snakes, sharp clawed insects and generous doses of leeches. On occasions morale was so low they all but threw in the towel. Finally, they reach their target, the Atlantic Ocean. They describe the euphoria of journey's end, mission accomplished. They camp out on the beach for three days just to savour the moment of triumph and digest the hardships endured. They gaze with wide-eyed wonder at hippopotamuses copulating in the breaking surf.

OK, that sounds like fun, but don't they want to have a warm bath, a cool beer, maybe a decent night's rest between clean sheets? Well, not really, it seems. One of them, the leader of the gang, declares misty-eyed he would like nothing better than to turn round and do the whole damn thing all over again.

Suddenly he has my total attention. Why on earth would any sane person repeat what was clearly a traumatic and a life-threatening ordeal? For the sake of science? No not that, for they already have whatever environmental data they intended to gather. So what is it? Another case of the RLS better-to-travel-hopefully-than-to-arrive syndrome?

I'm too tired to take this any further. Time for bed. I set my alarm to go off at 5.30 for I'm resolved not to miss the airport bus at 6.10 tomorrow morning. I fall asleep with visions of hippos humping to the rhythmic beat of the great Atlantic surf thumping down on the hard white sand of an African beach. I also have occasional sighting of a seriously large pair of lady's knickers scudding towards the far horizon.

Tuesday 26 September

Atisshoo! 2.37am. I must be catching a cold. Though actually I don't mind the sneezing. In fact, it's the best bit and really quite exciting this sudden paroxysm from head to tail leaving me all atremble. I once did a bit of research on the subject and came away disappointed with the banal explanation that a sneeze is merely a physical response to a nasal irritation.

Is that all it is? The average sneeze can reach speeds approaching 250 kph and sprays thousands of bacteria-filled droplets of moisture far and wide. So why does the whole body put all the force it can muster to create an almighty explosion of air through the nostrils for a mere tickle in the nose?

There must be something more to the humble sneeze. It's not expelling all those nasty bacteria at high speed just for us to be rid of them. It's doing its best to spread them to as many other people as possible along with sundry viral infections such as influenza, the common cold and worse. In short, the sneeze is potentially a lethal weapon trying to kill off the weakest and ensure the survival of the fittest.

On the other hand, the sneeze also has a more benign function as an early warning system which alerts the sneezer to the fact that temperatures have dropped to a level where catching a cold is a distinct possibility. All the sneezer then has to do is put on some warmer clothing or turn up the heating. Once this is done the body thermostat will be content and no further sneezes will be triggered.

So the sneeze is a subtle character and far more complex in its behaviour than one might expect. It's an ever vigilant friend to the body it protects while posing a potentially deadly threat to anyone else: two very different personalities for the price of one.

I lie awake waiting for the next sneeze but it doesn't come. Pretty soon I am asleep again. Then at 5.30am. the alarm clock goes off soon followed by a programmed phone call. My first thought is about the rain. I think I can hear it pelting down outside. But when I open the shutters it's only a strong wind rustling the leaves on the trees. Looks like the storm has almost blown itself out.

I have this feeling that travel days don't really count for much. If you wake up somewhere abroad with the knowledge you'll be back home later that day then a substantial part of you has in a sense already departed, gone on ahead of you. So you are not 100% there any more. This is especially true of early morning departures when there is precious little of the day to be savoured. However, I am determined not to sleepwalk my way to the airport but to take in fully whatever Bastia has to offer in the short time remaining.

Stepping out of *Hôtel Central* I feel energised by the early hour. There's always a magic to the pre-dawn, that brief moment when night is over and just before people are up. The city stirs but is not yet fully awake.

The freshly baked *croissant* aroma wafting deliciously out of *Maison Valéry* in *rue César Campinchi* is one of those potent signposts of French civilisation. Corsica may not be entirely reconciled to French rule but the bakery smells even in a politically radical city like Bastia are like an olfactory version of the national flag.

Likewise the *Bar de la Poste* could be anyway in continental France. Viewed from the street, its neon-lit interior feels like an aquarium with no water, one of those glass tanks in a zoo where lizards cling to rocks. A handful of non-communicating wan-faced nocturnal beings sit stoically still, hardly breathing, as if they'll need a dose of the sun's warming rays before they can move a muscle. I wonder if they have been waiting there all night in their clothes immobile as the subjects in an Edward Hopper canvas.

I also take note of some amazing double parking. Bad luck on those trapped if they want to make an early getaway. Even the pedestrian crossings are occupied by cars. Lights burn already in one or two small shops. *Les petits commerçants* putting in long hours and hard graft supplying the basic essentials of everyday life in France. The grit and sinew if not the backbone of the nation perhaps? I now turn into *avenue M. Sébastiani* where I stop to buy today's edition of *Corse-Matin* and take a quick picture of *Hôtel Univers* to begin my collection.

Up ahead I can make out *Rond Point Leclerc* and the *Préfecture* where in ten minutes the airport bus should depart. Glad to see I'm not the only passenger. A half dozen of us early birds stand patiently in the shadows like survivors of a disaster awaiting rescue. Silent nod of recognition with minimal eye contact is the standard greeting. No cheery *bonjour*, thank you very much. Shortly after 6 the bus pulls in.

We haul ourselves and luggage aboard, hand over 8 euros apiece and settle into our seats. At 6.05 the driver suddenly appears to lose patience with hanging around. With a shrug that says, if there's anyone else they should have been here by now, he shuts doors and hits the road a full five minutes ahead of schedule. With the next bus not due for more than three hours at 9.15 it certainly pays to show up well ahead of time.

The ride to the airport is uneventful as these things generally are. We pull up outside the terminal building at 6.50, so plenty of time to kill before my flight at 9.50. *Café crème* and *croissant* hit the spot. This elegant piece of pastry has become as much a French national symbol as a *béret* or *baguette*. Yet its true origins are not in France but Austria.

Since I have time on my hands, here's the story. During the Siege of Vienna in 1683 things had reached a critical point with the Turkish forces tunnelling under the city walls. But a sharp-eared Viennese baker heard the suspicious subterranean noises and raised the alarm. The attack was thwarted and soon after that the Turks withdrew. Vienna had survived.

In order to mark the heroic role of one of their own, the bakers of Vienna devised a pastry in the shape of the crescent symbol on the Turkish flag. The *croissant* finally reached France in 1770 when Marie-Antoinette introduced it to the French court following her marriage to Louis XVI.

So I consume my *croissant* with due regard for its proud history. It's a good specimen this one but I will not be sorry if it's the last I eat for a while. Breakfasting every day on bread and pastry does pall after a while.

That last comment makes me realise I'm winding down. Somehow each trip has its own inbuilt ration of energy to sustain it. Once that is used up and there's nothing left in the tank but fumes, exhaustion quickly follows. If someone were to ask me now to stay on for another day, then I would have to reply, sorry I can manage no more. At least not until I've refuelled, and that means going back to base.

Another reason for ending the trip now is that I'm running out of space in my A5 spiral bound *Pukka Pad*. I'm almost at the end of its 200 pages of premium quality writing paper. It feels as if that too has been carefully measured out in advance.

Still too early to check in, so I take an aimless stroll through the terminal. There's a stone in memory of *Antoine de Saint-Exupéry* the famous author-aviator who took off from Bastia's Poretta airport on 31 July 1944 and was never seen again.

Saint-Exupéry is best known for *Le Petit Prince*, a children's story also read by adults that tops the bill as France's all-time most popular book, selling a million copies a year worldwide in its hundred or so translations. I still struggle with its naïve, fairy-tale elements but the serious philosophical thoughts of the writer on the human condition are powerful stuff.

'For centuries, humanity has been descending an immense staircase whose top is hidden in the clouds and whose lowest steps are lost in a dark abyss. We could have ascended the staircase; instead we chose to descend it. Spiritual decay is terrible. . . There is one problem and only one in the world: to revive in people some sense of spiritual meaning. . ."

Can't be said much clearer than that.

In the context of travel writing *Antoine de Saint-Exupéry* exerted considerable influence albeit indirectly. For he travelled not in order to write, rather he let his travels inspire his writing. Nor were these of the voyage of discovery kind. They occurred in the course of his regular work as pilot on the pioneering airmail services in the 1920s and 30s which took him to far-flung places from the Andes to the Sahara. Usually flying on instinct rather than by instruments, *Saint-Exupéry* could get quite sniffy about the new planes with their more advanced navigational systems whose pilots he dismissed as being more like accountants than aviators.

The world *Saint-Exupéry* moved about in is now the very stuff of travel nostalgia: romantic airfields in exotic locations not characterless airports serving bland tourist resorts. It's not without irony that today's boom in travel and travel writing coincides with a global homogenisation of the travel experience.

What *Saint-Exupéry* would have to say about modern travel, we can only surmise. Speculation also surrounds the real cause of his premature death in what is generally presumed to be an aviation accident. No conclusive explanation has been offered, and given his published views about where the world and human civilisation were heading this raises the possibility of a suicide motivated by a dark sense of foreboding.

More gloomy thoughts call out from the cover of the news weekly *L'Express*: *FAUT-IL AVOIR HONTE D'ÊTRE FRANÇAIS?* So what is there for the French to be ashamed of? Quite a lot, it would appear. All the glory days of *la grande nation* are being re-examined. The film *Indigènes* has sparked off a national debate. It poses the question: did France cynically sacrifice her brave colonial troops during the country's liberation only to consign them afterwards to oblivion?

Among other historical accusations in the air is that Napoleon was guilty of genocide through the re-introduction of slavery. Another good reason I suppose why he had to be stopped. I wonder what *Saint-Exupéry* would have to say about all this. Would his traditionalist instincts prompt him to excuse the failings of the past? Or would the international humanist in him add his voice to the chorus of indictments?

I check in at the British Airways desk only to be told my name is not on the manifest. I'm not sure there is a manifest, because the young woman tells me there's *"un petit problème avec l'informatique."* Now, where have I heard that before? I produce an email confirming my reservation. She asks if she may keep it as a *"justificatif"* in case she's asked why she let me on the plane.

In the departure lounge I flick through today's *Corse-Matin*. Top story is that three people have gone missing while out on a picnic excursion in the hilly countryside near Ville di Pietrabugno. There's been no sign of them since Sunday. A major search and rescue operation is currently underway. As for the daily record of violence, there have been bomb attacks during the early hours of Monday morning on three banks in Propriano: *Caisse d'Épargne, Banque Populaire* and *Crédit Lyonnais*. The explosions were from home made devices and caused only modest damage. Robbery does not appear to be the motive since no attempt was made to steal money and the *dossier* has been promptly passed to the antiterrorist police in Paris.

I consult RG to find out what sort of place is Propriano. Apparently, this small ferry port 71km southwest of Ajaccio *"still has an unfinished appearance. This is due in part to terrorist bombs: the post office, a symbol of the French administration and especially targeted for its isolated position here, has had to be rebuilt four times after nationalist attacks."* So the Corsican cauldron continues to bubble.

BA6773 to London-Gatwick is called pretty much on time for its scheduled departure at 09.50. So it's goodbye to Corsica. I'll use the two hour flight to see what else *Corse-Matin* has to offer and let my thoughts settle. After take off my thoughts are soon back with *Saint-Exupéry* as I gaze down at the blue sea wondering at which point he met his watery grave.

The couple next to me is playing Scrabble. They look pretty good at it. Wonder if they can come up with an anagram for Corsica? I still can't manage one. Is there a special word for words that cannot be broken down as anagrams? Like the alphabetic equivalent of a prime number? But what purpose could that possibly serve? However, it's a thought nonetheless so I jot it down on the very last page of my notebook.

We land at Gatwick on schedule. I wait patiently along with the other passengers of BA6773 from Bastia for our various items of baggage to appear. Then we make our separate ways back to our sedentary lives. I think briefly of revisiting my, yes *my* armchair where I spent last Wednesday night. Surely it would look completely different in the context of me arriving rather than me departing? While still being exactly the same piece of furniture of course. I quickly decide that would be taking things too far in squeezing the last drop out of the travel experience.

I feel I have nothing more to report as I head back to central London on the *First Capital Connect* train. I pick up a copy of *Metro* and my eyes glide casually over familiar headlines that haven't changed that much during the few days of my absence. But they alight with interest on a reader's letter to the editor in which the correspondent declares, in response to a previous letter from another reader, that he refuses to grovel with respect for British culture.

Oh dear. It's like walking in on a family row. Our world is falling apart and all we seem to do is bicker among ourselves. Coming back even from such a short trip as this, I see things with the eyes of a stranger.

Trust the French to have a word for it, but they do. *Dépaysement* denotes the state of being outside one's usual surroundings or element, often in the sense of being lost, confused or all at sea. It comes from the verb *dépayser* which means literally to remove from one's country or to exile. So it's a condition that results from a temporary exile from the familiar.

So depending on how long you've been away your feeling of *dépaysement* can last for longer or shorter periods. In my case it's quickly spent. One glance at the *Metro* has brought me down to earth with a bump.

The next reminder that I am well and truly home is the *First Capital Connect* train which grinds to a halt somewhere in south London. The driver informs us of signal problems ahead at Moorgate and of consequent lengthy delays. I had been intending to go through to Kings Cross, but instead I hop off at London Bridge and catch a train to Charing Cross. Perhaps that's destiny playing a hand. In any case, it seems only right to end my journey where I began it.

I enjoy the grand approach across the Thames and alight at Charing Cross where I am amazed to see General Gordon and Reggie Baldwin resuming their conversation at the exact point they had reached last Wednesday on my way out.

RB: *Of course I can sell you a single to Khartoum, Sir. But with a Super Saver Off-peak Return, if you do decide to come back then you won't have to pay full whack all over again.*

GG: *I'll give you full whack if you don't get a move on.*

RB: *Only trying to be of service. So you're quite sure it's just a single to Khartoum, Sir?*

GG: *Yes, yes, yes! How many times do I have to tell you? A single will be quite enough on this occasion.*

RB: *Very well then, Sir. One single to Khartoum coming up. Permit me to wish you a very Bon Voyage, Sir.*

GG: *Thank you, my good man. Thank you.*

RB: *You can catch the train on platform 3, Sir. Change at London Bridge. Or you'll end up in Margate.*

The parallels between late 19th century Sudan and early 21st century Afghanistan strike me even more forcefully than before. But I'm too tired to go into that now. Outside the station I catch a 91 bus that takes me along the Strand to Aldwych then up Kingsway. I note a lively demonstration taking place outside the Civil Aviation Authority HQ, part of an environmental campaign against excessive flying.

I get off at Tavistock Square and nod a respectful greeting to the statue of Mahatma Gandhi sitting on his stone plinth in the middle of the garden. I cross the road and pass the exact spot outside the *British Medical Association* where at 9.47 am on 7 July 2005 a number 30 bus exploded, killing 14 people and injuring 110.

I got to know many of their faces from the missing persons posters that started going up on walls and hoardings within hours of the incident. Gandhi, a fervent believer in passive resistance rather than armed struggle and himself ultimately a victim of political violence, would have had a grandstand view of the bloodbath. From my study at home I heard the dull boom and then the shrill sirens that went on for hours.

I use this stop a lot and don't care to recall those terrible events. Today is different since I'm in writing mode. It's trivial stuff that lingers in the memory. The number 30 from Hackney to Marble Arch doesn't usually take this route. It had been diverted on account of the bombings on the Underground. But so what? A suicide bombing is by definition a rogue element, a random event. It will strike where it will.

What has become of the bomber Hasib Hussain? Has he been rewarded with his promised place in paradise for his heroic act of martyrdom, murder and mutilation? Many other bombs have fallen on London in the course of two World Wars leaving their own scar tissue if you know where to look. But those of 7 July 2005 are harder to deal with, coming as they did from people who were meant to be our fellow citizens.

Someone should be able to heal the wounds and bring this troubled world to its senses. It's not just religion pitted against religion. It's one sect of the same religion fighting another, neighbour killing neighbour. Do people really believe in the holiness of violence? Mahatma Gandhi, where are you now? Answer comes there none. All we have left is a statue in Tavistock Square. We are well and truly on our own.

Minutes later I am turning the key then pushing open the front door. The journey is over. Last thought is that perhaps the true purpose of travel is to make you appreciate home. Even a bad trip, especially a bad trip, can achieve that. After a pretty good one like this there is, in spite of physical fatigue, a rare sense of renewal, feeling refreshed and rebooted. So a good dose of travel can leave you both exhausted and energised.

That's something to ponder on. But what if you are not glad to be back? Then perhaps you may be living in the wrong place. I'm pleased to say that doesn't apply here. I'm happy to be home. So I shut the front door behind me and cease to be a traveller. Now where did I leave my slippers?

AFTERTHOUGHTS

So what was that all about? Why did I make that trip? What have I learned about travel? Why Corsica? To be frank, I'm not entirely sure I've actually been to Corsica. I mean the real Corsica. The island I visited might just as well have been an anagram: Rosicca, Accriso, Soccari, Carsico or Scaroci.

I think I would like to make a return trip and do some justice to the place and its people. I rather liked what I saw of Corsica, albeit distorted through the filter of my own preoccupations.

So for the time being it's questions and more questions rather than answers as I seek to make some sense of my Corsican travel diary. While I grapple with that from the familiar surroundings of home sweet home, some more general travel related matters present themselves for my attention.

Speaking at the World Travel Market in November 2006 US intelligence adviser Dr Marvin Cetron warned travel trade leaders that that they faced many uncertainties: *"The war on terror looks likely to go on for decades."* From a purely selfish, personal perspective, that's the rest of my life taken care of. But what is it like for young people growing up against this nightmare scenario? What happened to that lovely idea of peace through travel whereby wars would become obsolete as people got to know one another?

Terrorism isn't the only fly in the travel ointment. According to a report released in January 2007 by the European Commission global warming will leave Europe virtually unrecognisable in less than a century. Rising temperatures will bring an end to ski weekends and Mediterranean holidays as the snow and beaches disappear. Drought and desert will lay waste our dream landscapes in Provence and Tuscany.

As we look around to point the finger, the travel industry – yes, industry – cannot avoid its share of the blame. What started out as the most exciting benefit for humankind, the opportunity for ordinary mortals to see the wonders of the world, has become tarnished and besmirched. The very act of admiring the glories of Planet Earth has been sowing the seeds of destruction for what turns out to be a fragile and volatile habitat.

Suddenly, everything about travel is potentially suspect. Even green tourism, in as far as it involves air or road travel, is merely taking our polluting habits to areas of wilderness or natural beauty. We are sullying paradise with our nasty little carbon footprints. The barbarism is as shocking as Goths and Vandals sacking ancient Rome only with more lethal consequences. It's a depressing prospect and a cruel contrast to the idealised world of the travel brochures. There's a sense of loss as we start saying goodbye to all that

So what are the facts? *The Stern Review on the Economics of Climate Change* recently presented to the British Government included an emissions-by-sector pie chart showing that transportation accounts for 14%

of the problem. So cars and aeroplanes are key targets for reductions in greenhouse gases. Some people are responding. Richard Branson of Virgin Atlantic has pledged $3 billion to research into greener aviation, though cynics suggest the grounding of the airline's entire fleet would make better environmental sense.

Meanwhile, the aviation industry at large is booming. Phenomenal rates of expansion are predicted. Willie Walsh, British Airways CEO, responding to the challenge from the new anti-aviation pressure group *PLANE STUPID* declared: *"While it is crucial that aviation takes action on emissions, the notion that flying is a selfish, antisocial activity that single-handedly threatens planetary catastrophe bears no relation to evidence."*

The big oil corporation BP has been placing large press advertisements proudly announcing: *IT IS NOW POSSIBLE TO DRIVE IN NEUTRAL.* The idea is for individual motorists to carry on as before as long as they make a small annual payment towards renewable energy projects. Is this a smart conjuring trick to make our car emissions somehow vanish while we still drive around in the same cars burning the same fuels that are causing the problem in the first place? But the one clear fact to emerge here is BP's admission that road users generate 22% of the UK's CO^2 emissions.

Typical of the shock headlines following *The Stern Review* is in *The London Paper* of 30 October 2006: *A LAST CHANCE TO SAVE THE PLANET.*

Of course, it's not the planet that needs saving. It's us. For once we humans have made the earth uninhabitable for ourselves, then it follows that the carbon emissions we create will fall dramatically and nature will then set about restoring the balance over thousands and thousands of years which is the timescale over which these things work. The 10 to 15 years we are now presented with as a window in which to turn things around seems hugely optimistic.

In this new age of carbon awareness the writing must be on the wall for all those cheap flights that have been responsible for millions of extra air passenger miles over the last decade, including my own frequent trips, most recently to Corsica.

So where does that leave the travel industry and its supporting chorus of travel writers? I buy a copy of *The Sunday Times* vaguely expecting to find Colin Thubron still working his way along the *Silk Road*. But instead, occupying prime slot in the Travel Section is Jeremy Clarkson. Now there's an interesting case.

For those not familiar, Clarkson is a leading exponent of the big gob school of journalism, mouthing off about whatever takes his fancy. His stock-in-trade is to offend for a cheap laugh. He's good at it. The job isn't properly done unless serious offence is given. He may come across as a clown or buffoon but no one should accuse Clarkson, as some do, of having half a brain. Though it may be true he only uses half of it most of the time. But that's the way his paymasters want him. For he wouldn't be half as funny were he actually to think too long about what he is saying.

What's relevant here is that Clarkson has taken a lot of flak for his unrepentant celebration of the internal combustion engine. Indeed, he has delighted in his role as *bête noire* of the environmental lobby, sticking up two fingers to anyone who dares suggest his precious motor cars are anything less than God's gift to humanity.

For a quick taste of the Clarkson approach to green issues here's an extract from a story published only a week before the polar bear became listed as an endangered species on account of melting icecaps.

"I don't mind if you want to buy a 4x4, I really don't. I think you're a bit of a loony if you have one in central London, but would I stop you? No. Because it's no skin off my nose, and even if it is true that you're making the world hotter, good frankly. I like it when it's warm. This summer was lovely and if the world's petrolheads and school run mums helped create that, I think we should pat ourselves on the back."

So here we have Clarkson the travel writer on safari in Botswana. Very funny he is too, cocking a snook at the nature-is-wonderful scripts of all those wildlife documentaries. His smart angle is to tell us how bad the animal kingdom smells and how ridiculous are some of God's creatures, all amply illustrated with an inventory of everything that made him laugh.

"The time I laughed most at a hippo was when we ran one over in our speedboat."

It's vintage Clarkson, ending with a list of things that did impress him, only to set up his final blow:

"But towering above these things were the Yamaha quad bikes we used to cross the Makgadikgadi salt pans…"

This is frightfully amusing. I can just picture the scene. Vroom! Vroom! Jeremy Clarkson burning fuel and rubber with gay abandon, drowning out David Attenborough's reverential whispers about the natural wonders of the African outback. I chuckle briefly at his description of the hyena as a *"biblically ugly dog-cat"* but then I stop to ask myself what's going on here. What is the connection in his mind between the Bible and ugliness? It's a curious throwaway line, almost as if Clarkson wants to demonstrate his skill with words, turning even an adverb into an oblique insult.

Anyway, knowing what a good sport he is, I'm sure Clarkson won't mind if the hyena exercises his right of reply by telling his mates via the bush telegraph that he's recently seen a human being with a face like a wildebeest's arse, a truly hilarious example of a *homo* not so *sapiens*. By now they're splitting their sides over that one all the way from the Cape to Cairo. I know, pretty childish. But that's hyenas for you. They will laugh at anything and can't stop to save their lives.

Getting back to global warming, if the scientific evidence about carbon emissions is correct, and that's now a 90% probability according to the most cautious opinions, then burning fossil fuels for fun is not really that funny any more. So the same must go for Jeremy Clarkson's stuff-the-environment brand of journalism which becomes less and less amusing along with the melting of those ice caps and glaciers he has done his best to deny and now glibly to promote, albeit with his tongue firmly in cheek. Or is it?

Let's not be too gloomy. Why not think the unthinkable? How about Clarkson's car breaking down on the road to Damascus? Then he will see the light and go forth to preach the green gospel. Among his disciples will be Michael Schumacher, another celebrity petrolhead and arch carbon villain. Together they could lead a campaign for health warnings to be posted on cars: *THIS VEHICLE IS KILLING THE PLANET.*

Instead of this highly improbable fantasy, we have super-dimensional billboards of Clarkson leering at us over toxic traffic jams like an avenging angel of doom. The high priest of internal combustion urges motorists to keep on driving come hell or high water, both of which may well be on the cards. But what if it turns out that global warming is a natural phenomenon and it makes no difference how much carbon we humans spew out? Well, they'll have to invent a new verb to describe the horrendous sound of Clarkson crowing from dawn to dusk and long into the night.

Assuming however that conventional wisdom is correct and we are in fact destroying our environment, then travel writers as well as motoring correspondents have to ask themselves some searching questions. I mean all this endless encouragement of countless others to fly or drive here, there and everywhere for no good reason. So for how much longer in the emerging green society will we be permitted to ply our irresponsible trade? Perhaps, we might be forced to seek a new *raison d'être* creating imaginary journeys for armchair travellers as a harmless substitute for the real thing.

The idea of travel by proxy is not new. In the Middle Ages, when getting about was slow, dangerous and unreliable, those with the means sometimes paid others to make those soul-saving pilgrimages on their behalf to Rome, Canterbury or Santiago de Compostela. Applying that principle to modern requirements, each of the new breed of surrogate traveller could conceivably represent hundreds of stay-at-homes, perhaps carrying cardboard cut-outs of their sedentary clients to be snapped as photo souvenirs posed in front of Niagara Falls and the Taj Mahal.

Digital technology can also be used to produce DVDs simulating walks in the Black Forest or surfing in Hawaii, all in the comfort of your own living room. The possibilities are endless. There should be plenty of scope for writers and photographers supplying material for this new industry of virtual travel.

Environmental concerns aside, travel writers could take a more robust stance in other ways. Critical faculties are often suspended when composing well mannered travel articles. During my brief stay in Corsica it was on average a bomb a day. Great title for a travel story. But would a travel editor ever use it? In any case, I too would consider it misleading since I felt pretty safe wherever I went in Corsica. Oh dear, is that me being well mannered again? The point is I wouldn't get away with it even if I wanted to. Always look for the positives is the rule of travel journalism. We really want people to follow in our footsteps to far-flung places.

Guide book writers can get away with more critical stuff. Consider this tasty offering in the *Cadogan Guide to Provence* by Dana Facaros and Michael Pauls:

"For proof that Provencal sunlight softens the Anglo-Saxon brain, consider St-Maximin. 'Considerable charm', gushes one guidebook; 'another pretty Provencal village', yawns another. Prosper Mérimée, back in 1834, got it right: 'Saint-Maximin is a miserable hole between Aix and Draguignan.' It hasn't changed. The general atmosphere of bricks and litter is reminiscent of some burnt-out inner-city in the Midlands or Midwest. It is hard to imagine a place remaining in such a state of total, lackadaisical decrepitude, in the midst of a prosperous region, without some effort of will on the part of its inhabitants."

Defying this, or possibly inspired by it, I once made a perfectly enjoyable overnight stay in St-Maximin and couldn't make much sense of this stinking review. But then I tend to feel more at ease in unpretentious places. Prettified villages with effusive write-ups often have me running for the exit. So for me St-Maximin-de-la-Ste-Baume, to give the place its full name, was really ok. Even if it had been awful, why should I hold that against it? I fully accept the inalienable right of places to be run down and falling apart, also of the natives to be surly slackers. But if they promote themselves as lovely tourist destinations then I suppose it's fair game.

For hotels, because their mission is to welcome travellers, it's always been open season. Richard Ford, described with acerbic wit the inn at Alhama de Granada in *Murray's Handbook for Spain* of 1845:

"The posada at Alhama, albeit called La Grande, is truly iniquitous; diminutive indeed are the accommodations, colossal the inconveniences. [...] All who are wise will bring from Málaga a good hamper of eatables, a bota of wine, and some cigars, for however devoid of creature comforts this grand hotel, there is a grand supply of creeping creatures, and the traveller runs the risk of bidding adieu to sleep..."

Expectations have risen considerably since the pioneering days of the Arab traveller Ibn Battuta who set off in 1325 with little money from his home town of Tangiers to make a pilgrimage to Mecca. After that he just kept on travelling for nigh on thirty years driven by an insatiable curiosity. Only when it was all over did he sit down and dictate an account of his experiences. Ibn Battuta had his low moments when he must have pondered the meaning of his presence in some alien, unwelcoming place. Doubtless he asked himself the same question that Bruce Chatwin used for the title of his book: *What Am I Doing Here?*

Whatever hardships they may endure, today's professional travel writers can always remind themselves they are essentially at work. Furthermore, they never walk alone, for they are accompanied by a constant awareness of an invisible audience of readers waiting eagerly on their report. So their purpose is not for a moment in doubt. Everything that happens to them is potential material for their stories.

So where do we get this desire to flit about the world and pass comment on whatever and wherever we please? For travel writing can hardly be described as a universal activity. Do we find Mongolian horsemen and Bedouin tribesmen trekking up the M1 to relate impressions of Birmingham and Bletchley to their compatriots back home? Or perhaps we aren't folkloric or exotic enough to merit outside interest?

Going back to those mad buggers in the *National Geographic* who, having crossed the most terrifying bit of equatorial Africa, could think of nothing better than to turn round and do it all over again. What is that all about? In their case travel has become an end in itself, a way of life, an addiction, a recreational drug. Stop and you get withdrawal symptoms. But travel is more of a mind drug than a physical dependency. It induces a rare state of excitement to be savoured and enjoyed along with all the lovely new faces and places.

For when you are on the road, it's the eternal heartbeat of the big wide world you tune in to. You are defined against a mighty canvas: the Himalayas, the Grand Canyon, the Great Barrier Reef. You are part of the bigger picture, absorbed back into the common ancestry of the human race. It's no longer just you in your little box facing your individual destiny all alone. There are others out there living their lives. You meet them and quickly realise we are all in this together.

When travelling you don't feel you're getting old in quite the same way. Somehow, you defy the passage of time. Yes, travel can make you immortal. For it's only when you get home and put on your slippers that transience begins again and the ageing process resumes its inevitable march towards oblivion. When you sit on your sofa in your own living room you hear and see the clock ticking away the seconds and years of your own life. It can of course be argued all this is a delusion, that travel cannot arrest or even slow the passing of time. But if the traveller experiences it otherwise while being engaged in the act of travel, then it's real enough.

When you are on the move, you are oriented to the future, aiming to get to the next town, to eat the next meal, to visit the next castle and so on. The clock always points the traveller forward with planes to catch, places to see, people to meet. The act of looking back, unless you are partial to the Maori View, forms no part of it as long as you are underway.

This bright horizon towards which we constantly strive becomes our continuous future in the present, an excitingly novel tense for conjugating verbs. We enter a new time dimension in which the world we are passing through remains eternally fresh and young. Change and decay only happen to those who stay behind.

Of material possessions it is rightly said that you cannot take them with you. But with travel you can and you do. All those journeys you have made in your life accompany you on that last great voyage into the unknown. They form an essential part of everything that has made you who you are.

If all that sounds a bit abstract, a more tangible property of travel is that it lifts you out of your daily cares and concerns. It takes your mind off tiresome things. The world becomes a stage for you the traveller to strut your stuff without attachment to any particular place. You are transient, drifting, in suspense, detached from all the hassles of being rooted. You defy the restrictions and limitations on your person that come with a settled existence: from leaking roofs to nasty brown envelopes. All that boring stuff is put on hold. You float serenely above the surface of harsh reality. Just passing through. Nothing sticks. You are coated in *Teflon*. An extraterrestrial. Not from here.

Isn't this exactly what Kenneth Grahame's *Toad* experienced in *The Wind in the Willows* on his first encounter with the motor car?

"Glorious, stirring sight! The poetry of motion! The real way to travel! The only way to travel! Here today – in next week tomorrow! Villages skipped, towns and cities jumped – always somebody else's horizon! O bliss! O poop-poop! O my! O my!"

Always somebody else's horizon. That's exactly what I've just spent a couple of paragraphs trying to say in my own words. Yes, I finally have to admit it. For me travel makes the world go round. It really does, and writing about it is the icing on the cake. Accordingly, I must end up after all by agreeing with Robert Louis Stevenson when he writes:

"I travel not to go anywhere, but to go. I travel for travel's sake. The great affair is to move."

However, it doesn't seem fair to let RLS have the last word as well as the first in what is after all my book. Nor do I feel fully qualified to claim that honour for myself. So perhaps the best way to bring this rambling discussion on the purpose and nature of travel to some kind of conclusion is to open the final pages to a miscellany of voices not already quoted in this account. These are from various countries and periods, but each one is very much of an individual personality with something specific to say.

Before I hand over I'd like to correct or qualify something I said earlier about leaving yourself behind when you travel. On reflection, it's not that simple. People who try to throw off one persona and grab another are not convincing in any guise.

Besides, especially when you travel solo it can get lonely with no one to commune with. So I'll reverse my earlier advice and thoroughly recommend that you do take yourself along, but only on condition that the two of you use the opportunity to get to know one another better. This is often much easier in unfamiliar foreign surroundings. And finally, don't be afraid of talking to yourself from time to time. It's the first sign of sanity.

SOME VIEWS ON THE ART OF TRAVEL

"Experience, travel — these are as education in themselves."
Euripides

"Though we travel the world over to find the beautiful, we must carry it with us or we find it not."
Ralph Waldo Emerson

"I see my path, but I don't know where it leads. Not knowing where I'm going is what inspires me to travel it."
Rosalia de Castro

"The real voyage of discovery consists not in seeking new landscapes but in having new eyes."
Marcel Proust

"A man travels the world in search of what he needs and returns home to find it."
George Moore

"Make voyages! Attempt them... there's nothing else."
Tennessee Williams

"The fool wanders, a wise man travels."
Thomas Fuller

"Like all great travellers, I have seen more than I remember, and remember more than I have seen."
Benjamin Disraeli

"The whole object of travel is not to set foot on foreign land; it is at last to set foot on one's own country as a foreign land."
G. K. Chesterton

"It is better to travel alone than with a bad companion."
African Proverb

"I set out alone, finding no companion to cheer the way with friendly intercourse, and no party of travellers with whom to associate myself."
Ibn Battuta

"It will be all over this day week - comfort - discomfort; and the zest and rush that no engagements, hours, habits give. Then we shall take them up again with more than the zest of travelling."
Virginia Woolf

"He travels best that knows when to return."
Thomas More

"Paths are made by walking."
Franz Kafka [ascribed]

"Men travel faster now, but I do not know if they go to better things."
Willa Sibert Cather

"I never travel without my diary. One should always have something sensational to read in the train."
Oscar Wilde

"If you wish to travel far and fast, travel light. Take off all your envies, jealousies, unforgiveness, selfishness and fears."
Cesare Pavese

"I would like to spend the whole of my life travelling, if I could anywhere borrow another life to spend at home."
William Hazlitt

"Whether you travel or you stay at home by the fireside, you will inevitably reach an age when life is no more than a routine habit in whatever surrounding suits you best."
Honoré de Balzac

"Twenty years from now you will be more disappointed by the things that you didn't do than by the ones you did do. So throw off the bowlines. Sail away from the safe harbor. Catch the trade winds in your sails. Explore. Dream. Discover."
Mark Twain

"Most travel is best of all in the anticipation or the remembering; the reality has more to do with losing your luggage."
Regina Nadelson

"When I wish to be misinformed about a country, I ask the man who has lived there thirty years."
Lord Palmerston

"Travel is the most private of pleasures. There is no greater bore than the travel bore. We do not in the least want to hear what he has seen in Hong Kong."
Vita Sackville-West

"Travel is an art and one must practice it in a relaxed way, with passion and love."
Tiziano Terzani

"People travel to wonder at the height of the mountains, at the huge waves of the seas, at the long course of the rivers, at the vast compass of the ocean, at the circular motion of the stars, and yet they pass by themselves without wondering."
Saint Augustine

"But why, oh why, do the wrong people travel, when the right people stay at home?"
Noel Coward

"Our battered suitcases were piled on the sidewalk again; we had longer ways to go. But no matter, the road is life."
Jack Kerouac

"To awaken alone in a strange town is one of the pleasantest sensations in the world."
Freya Stark

"One's destination is never a place, but a new way of seeing things."
Henry Miller

"Bits of this place (Lebanon) will come back with me, because journeys never end."
Brian Keenan

"No matter where you go, there you are."
Unknown

"Now that my journeys east and west are done, there is one last corner left, my grave."
Ibn Battuta

PS

It seems I am to have the last word after all. For my Corsican journey has since produced more than I bargained for. Those super size knickers I saw break free so spectacularly during that big storm over Bastia have given birth as it were to a short story I've chosen to call *Mrs Mulroony's Fly-Away French Bloomers*.

As the title may suggest this is not a serious work of literature that I could easily read out loud to worthy members past or present of the Bloomsbury group. So although I would not expect Virginia Woolf to find in it much, if any merit, I hope she would at least commend me for following her advice to keep faith with writing as something worth doing for its own good sake.

But why Mrs Mulroony and not some Corsican lady as the owner of the fly-away bloomers? Well, I felt it appropriate to move the story from Bastia to London in order to use a more familiar setting for the various unbelievable adventures that take place.

For if Virginia Woolf may permit herself to transport a whole lighthouse all the way from Cornwall to Scotland, why should I not convey a mere pair of French knickers from the shores of the Mediterranean to the banks of the Thames? Surely that also falls within the scope of what travel writing can achieve.

www.ingramcontent.com/pod-product-compliance
Lightning Source LLC
Chambersburg PA
CBHW022102160426
43198CB00008B/327